| DATE | | | |
|---|---|---|---|
| | | | |
| | | | |
| | | | |
| | | | |
| | | | |
| | | | |
| | | | |
| | | | |

*Television Westerns*

# Television Westerns

*Major and Minor Series,*
*1946–1978*

*by*
Richard West

McFarland & Company, Inc., Publishers
*Jefferson, North Carolina, and London*

Library of Congress Cataloguing-in-Publication Data

West, Richard, 1946–
  *Television westerns.*

  Includes index.
  1. Westerns (Television programs)—United States—
History and criticism. I. Title.
PN1992.8.W4W47   1987        791.45′09′093278        87-42525

ISBN 0-89950-252-0 (acid-free natural paper) ∞

Printed in the United States of America.

McFarland & Company, Inc., Publishers
  Box 611, Jefferson, North Carolina 28640

# Acknowledgments

Special thanks to Frank and Vivian Barning of *Baseball Hobby News*, who gave a would-be writer his first major break, and to Jim Beckett of Beckett Publications for helping me overcome a severe case of writer's block which had lasted entirely too long. Thanks also to my parents, who although they aren't around to see the end product would be pleased to know that something other than eyestrain came out of countless hours of TV watching. And last, but by no means least, thanks to all the major and minor actors who appeared in the seemingly countless TV Westerns and who helped make the 1950s and 1960s such a wonderful time in which to be alive.

# Contents

# Introduction

They came riding into America's living rooms in one form or another from the earliest days of television and rode off into the sunset in the 1970s. TV critics more often than not treated them with disdain, when they would even condescend to discuss them at all, since they weren't "art" (much like the movie critics who think your favorite movie is trash if it isn't a foreign production with subtitles being the only way you can understand the dialogue). But, if you grew up in the 1950s and early 1960s, they more than likely represented your television heroes, these gun-totin' denizens of the Old West. And there were lots to choose from: 119 different network series, many of which had several possible heroes. Toss in the syndicated series and you were probably closer to 150 programs and 200 heroes.*

It seems the American people have always had a love affair with the cowboy from the earliest days of filmmaking. Thus when the programming moguls in charge of early television were looking for someone or something to fill out their schedules, the cowboy was there to lead the way. The Lone Ranger was popular on radio, so why couldn't he make the transition to television? After all, there was a ready-made

---

*Not counting the 1980s attempts at returning Westerns to the small screen, the myriad of syndicated series, and those which weren't truly Westerns such as "Little House on the Prairie," a total of 119 Westerns appeared in prime time during the Golden Age of TV Westerns, a period spanning approximately the years of 1950–75, although there were several which came before and after those years. If one were to toss in trashy situation comedies such as "F Troop," which was set in the West, then the schmaltzy "Little House" was a Western and so was "I Love Lucy."

Of the 119 different Westerns, ABC was the leader with 53, NBC was right behind with 47, and CBS brought up the rear with a mere 29. Since that total comes to 129, something isn't right, but some series, such as "Wagon Train," were on two networks and are thus counted twice.

audience. Ditto "Gunsmoke," although there was no way William Conrad, who with his mellifluous tones had thrilled radio listeners as Matt Dillon, could come across effectively on TV. Matt Dillon just did not weigh in at 300 pounds! So James Arness, fresh from playing the monster in the original movie version of "The Thing," was recruited, and what resulted was the longest-running Western in television history.

While Chester A. Riley and Ralph Kramden were popular and lovable schnooks in that era, the Westerns were in their glory and virtually ruling the airwaves. It was a time when heroes were needed. World War II and Korea were still a bit too fresh in everyone's mind to glamorize wartime adventures as the networks were to do in the '60s with programs such as "Combat" and "The Rat Patrol," so the heroes came instead from a safer period of history—the Old West. The kids had Davy Crockett, Zorro, Wild Bill, Jingles, and Annie Oakley; the whole family could find heroes in the likes of Paladin and Wyatt Earp.

Did it really make any difference if Wild Bill Hickok was portrayed as being clean-shaven, resplendent in his buckskin outfit, when the real Wild Bill had hair down to his shoulders, a drooping mustache, and was more gambler than marshal? Of course not! Or how about Davy Crockett, who appeared on the Disney series as anything but the uncouth, shaggy, bearded, semiliterate braggart he really was? Fess Parker portrayed Old Davy as squeaky-clean, complete with the slicked-down hair everyone wore in the '50s, and no one really cared. As far as it went, Fess Parker *was* Davy Crockett, just as Hugh O'Brian was really Wyatt Earp.

By the time the mid- to late '60s rolled around, things began to change as the youngsters of the '50s and early '60s became teenagers and young adults. Heroes became passé—or at least heroes who rode horses and tamed the West. Those of us living in those times liked to think we had become sophisticated; we just weren't into cowboys and shoot-'em-ups anymore. The young people who revelled in the adventures of the Lone Ranger and his faithful Indian companion now revelled in the adventures of the Beatles and worried about whether they would be sent to a place called Viet Nam, where the bad guys were the Viet Cong, who used real bullets. It was no longer a case of the good guys in white hats going up against the bad guys in black. In short, life was no longer simple and uncomplicated; if you still thought it was, you grew up in a hurry when you found out your friendly local draft board had classified you 1-A.

The time for hero-worship was past. Everyone had been shocked by the Kennedy and King assassinations and the treatment Blacks received as they fought for their civil rights. Everyone in television's target age group wanted programs that helped raise the social consciousness; forget about a bunch of guys riding their horses and rescuing the damsel in distress! The big question suddenly became, is it socially relevant? And cowboys just didn't fit into that particular frame of reference. As a result, the Westerns that still remained faded into oblivion one by one, the victim of low ratings. They haven't made a comeback since.

Periodically, one of the networks will make a feeble attempt at resurrecting those simpler times before every home had a computer, but the day of the cowboy on television has long since passed. You need only look at recent attempts to return the oaters to the small screen to see that people are more interested in the sexual shenanigans of the "Dallas" and "Dynasty" bunch, or the essentially impossible family situations presented by the new breed of situation comedies, than in cowboys. TV executives even tried to bring back Bret Maverick in the '80s for the benefit of those of us who refused to let the '50s and early '60s rest in peace, but poor Bret wound up as a mere shadow of his former self and was soon gone. And a modern Western, "The Yellow Rose," tried incorporating elements of the Western and the prime-time soap opera into one, only to die after less than a full season. The general rule today seems to be, if they live on a ranch or ride a horse, forget it. Ranches mean cowboys and cowboys are no longer the in thing, even if they drive a pick-up more than they ride a horse and they take the girl to bed instead of bedding down with Old Paint. Cowboys? Too childish in the '80s.

Ask anyone who has watched television to any extent—and that takes in just about everyone—and they will tell you that television programming is cyclical. For a time, Westerns were the big-ticket item; then came situation comedies, cops and robbers, adventure and drama shows, and soap operas. Today the prime-time soap operas, after ruling the roost for a number of years, seem to be waning. But today's values for programs dictate they either be funny or have soap-operaish plots continuing from week to week and year to year in a never-ending foray of sexual escapades, many of which are ludicrous in their lack of reality. And we mustn't forget the fact that the people have to be rich. Not just rich, but filthy rich. Fabulously wealthy, as a matter of fact, which is something the Western heroes most assuredly were not. Some were to a certain extent in the so-called "adult Westerns," where Paladin lived a life of luxury in his opulent San Francisco hotel. The Cartwrights never seemed to have any monetary problems either, and Yancy Derringer wasn't exactly a pauper. But for every Paladin, you had two Lucas McCains. For every Yancy Derringer, there was a Bret Maverick who dropped a pile of money at the card tables and subsequently found it necessary to leave town in the middle of the night to escape his creditors. And for every Ben Cartwright who slept in very comfortable surroundings, there were three Johnny Yumas who used their saddles for pillows and slept under the stars. Cowboys weren't supposed to be rich, and at night they preferred the company of their horses to that of the curvaceous blond.

Given the tastes of today's television viewer, if the Western were to be introduced today as the latest TV craze, we would probably wind up with "Gunsmoke" being retitled "Dodge City," with the basic story line being, "Matt Dillon is the sheriff of Dodge City and Kitty Russell his wealthy lady friend who operates the Long Branch Casino. Matt, Kitty, and Deputy Chet Goode, a closet homosexual, are embroiled weekly in liaisons that center around the odd sexual habits of certain Dodge City characters."

If sitcoms are the wave of the future, choosing to make "Gunsmoke" a situation comedy might result in its being retitled "Kitty's Place," where "Matt Dillon, the good-natured sheriff of Dodge City, becomes embroiled in heart-warming situations in his attempts to help the various townspeople who drop by his lady friend Kitty Russell's restaurant. His adopted son Chester, crippled in a car wreck that took his parents' lives, usually becomes embroiled in a scheme of some sort, the end result being that he learns a valuable lesson about growing up."

"Bonanza" might wind up with the same title, but with a somewhat different story line, to wit: "The escapades of a dictatorial father, Ben Cartwright, and his three sons: Adam, a con artist who is out to get his father's timber fortune by hook or crook; Hoss, a simple-minded but well-meaning dolt who causes the family shame when he's let off their palatial estate; and Joe, a former priest who is tortured by the thought that he made a girl pregnant and who, when not working in the family-owned bank, spends his spare time trying to find her."

As a sitcom, "Bonanza" might wind up as "'Ben and His Boys': The story of Ben Cartwright, a widower with three sons: Adam, a struggling young lawyer; Hoss, a slightly retarded teenager; and Little Joe, a high school senior who is the captain of the football team. The misadventures they run into each week provide often semi-inspirational messages to the audience once the weekly crisis is resolved."

"The Big Valley" would no doubt wind up as a matriarchal version of "Dallas"; need more be said?

To those of us who were weaned on the good guys vs. the bad guys, these modern-day possibilities seem like heresy. You just couldn't tamper with Matt, the Cartwrights or the Barkleys (now *they* were fabulously wealthy, but they also came along near the end of the line for the Westerns); they have to remain unsullied and untainted by bed-hopping and other dastardly deeds. And somehow the thought of making Matt Dillon the leading character in a situation comedy almost smacks of blasphemy. The Westerns were meant to be simple and uncomplicated, and they would not succeed in any other form.

Obviously, not all of the Westerns were as successful as "Gunsmoke," "Wanted: Dead or Alive," or even "Cimarron Strip." For every one of those series which lasted a minimum of one season in prime time, there was a "Young Dan'l Boone," which lasted a mere four weeks in 1977. Some of them, such as "How the West Was Won," which featured a post–Matt Dillon James Arness, are remembered somewhat fondly; they were the victims of low ratings or were cancelled for other unknown reasons, and we never truly had the opportunity to know the characters and enjoy the series. Others, such as "Tate," are barely remembered — if they're remembered at all. A total of 31 such series appeared in prime-time (another, which is not listed, the "Wildside Chamber of Commerce" — later "Wildside" — appeared in 1985 and is thus not considered to have appeared in the Golden Age of TV Westerns), and it is possible you might remember some of them. They range from "The Barbary Coast," with San Francisco of the 1870s as its background to "Young Dan'l Boone," traversing the frontier of the late 1700s and early 1800s. Most of them featured the standard formula of the good guys and bad guys riding the plains, and while it's not possible to say much about them, one thing can be said about them all: They died with their boots on.

On the other end of the spectrum, only two lasted more than 10 years. "Gunsmoke" hung on for 20 years, a longevity record exceeded by only four other shows in television history. "The Tonight Show" with all its hosts and name changes (Jack Paar, "America After Dark," etc.), Walt Disney and its various offspring ("Wonderful World of Disney," etc.), "The Ed Sullivan Show," and "The Red Skelton Show."

"Bonanza" hung around for 14 years, a record exceeded only by the aforementioned and nine others, "Meet the Press," "What's My Line," "Lassie," "The Lawrence Welk Show," "Kraft Television Theatre," "I've Got a Secret," "The Jack Benny Show," "Jackie Gleason" (including "The Honeymooners" and other names), "The Perry Como Show," and "60 Minutes." "Meet the Press," still on the air, is the longest continuously running show, but spent only 18 of its 38 years in prime-time, and there are no doubt countless local programs and soap operas which have been on an equal length of time. That master of countrified corn-pone humor, "Hee Haw," is rapidly closing in on the 20-year mark, but most of its time on the air has been spent in syndication.

Sharing the 14-year circle with the Cartwrights were "Ozzie and Harriet," "Armstrong Circle Theatre," and "The Gillette Cavalcade of Sports." Considering the myriad of shows which have appeared since the introduction of prime-time network telecasting in 1946, that's pretty select company.

Meanwhile, there were some programs that could be counted upon to last a varying number of years, and they showed up just about anywhere and at any time, not to mention those that were here today and gone at the same time. Some of them were on in the afternoons, some in the evenings, some on weekends, and many rode the range on independent stations. It wasn't that they weren't good—many of them were much better than some of the programs served up by the networks such as "My Mother, the Car" and "Me and the Chimp." But the fact is they never showed up on any network's schedule. Some were produced strictly for sale to whichever station wanted them, while others originally started out as network series but suddenly found themselves bumped at the last minute in favor of something else. "Union Pacific," for example, was set to begin its westward run on CBS in 1958, but none of the episodes ever found their way onto the network. As with other genre programs, however, syndication of Westerns helped keep the actors starring in them employed, and they proved to be a boon for both the independent stations looking for something other than old movies and for network affiliates who were in the market to fill out a half-hour on Saturday afternoon. While there were more syndicated series in existence than J.R. Ewing has devious plots to do whatever it is he's been trying to do for all these years, there are few records available today about these series, and what is available is sketchy at best.

Syndication today plays a major role in keeping the Western alive. Most of the former network programs are available (providing residual checks for the actors who starred in the series), and the formerly syndicated shows are still around today in the same form, providing a staple for cable networks and independent stations alike. If you're wondering where they all went, on cable your best bet is the Christian Broadcasting Network (believe it or not!), which offers a steady dose of series on weekends and periodically during the early evening hours weeknights.

The USA Network also offers Westerns, primarily on Sunday evenings, and like CBN runs a large number of non–Western series as well. In addition, numerous series from the Golden Age of Westerns appear frequently on the so-called Superstations, particularly WTBS (Atlanta) and WGN (Chicago), but they often appear at ridiculous hours and have a tendency to be last-minute fill-ins between the conclusion of the baseball game and the start of the wrestling matches.

The Disney studios chose to keep their series out of syndication, but for the person willing to pay the money to his local cable company, reruns of all the Disney classics appear frequently on the Disney Channel.

Two words of warning: One, be prepared to sit through an interminable number of commercials approximately every six minutes (except on Disney). Two, be prepared for a letdown. Often they aren't as good as you may remember their being.

In the listings that follow, the theme music or song is listed along with the original artist and record label so that should you desire, you can search through the record bins at the Salvation Army Store, Goodwill, or record collector's conventions, looking for the theme song to "The Saga of Andy Burnette" as recorded by the series star, Jerome Courtland. In some instances, recorded theme music is not the original recording played over the credits, but does present a passable cover where the original was never issued on record. Many of these, incidentally, appeared on RCA's Children's Bluebird label and were generally done by the Sons of the Pioneers or the Prairie Chiefs.

To those of us who grew up in that far simpler time before Viet Nam, before Nixon and Watergate, before disco and punk rock, before those god-awful music videos and home computers, this book is dedicated. And almost certainly to Matt, Davy, Major Adams, Bret, Bart, and all the others who made those days such a pleasant time in which to spend our youth.

# The Shows

## The Adventures of Davy Crockett

On Wednesday, October 27, 1954, Walt Disney's "Disneyland" took to the air and shortly became the first major hit series on ABC as the result of a shrewd move (actually pure genius) by Disney. On December 15 of that year, Disney aired the first of three episodes to appear under the "Frontierland" banner, with Fess Parker starring as frontiersman Davy Crockett. For anyone — particularly kids — around at that time, things were never quite the same after that.

One of the basic tenets of the Disney philosophy was that everything had to be wholesome, and "The Adventures of Davy Crockett" was. Turning a less-than-wholesome braggart of a frontiersman into an American hero and legend, Disney's production gave birth to a short-lived, but major, industry that saw everything from coonskin caps to Davy Crockett bubble gum cards, a complete set of one series in Mint condition now bringing about $75 in the collector's market while the scarcer second series in the same condition brings about $150. The gum was terrible, but kids chewed it; they also collected the cards, wore coonskin caps, carried Davy Crockett lunchboxes, and wrote on a Davy Crockett tablet at school, no doubt using a Davy Crockett pencil.

Taking an unknown actor and making him the star of a series took guts, but neither Disney nor Parker was sorry. Prior to becoming Crockett, Parker had played a few bit parts here and there in various movies and was first spotted by Disney playing just such a part in the science-fiction movie "Them." Unknown? Other than to his agent, Parker was definitely that.

Ole Davy started off with just three one-hour episodes: "Davy Crockett, Indian Fighter" (December 15, 1954); "Davy Crockett Goes

9

to Congress" (January 26, 1955) and "Davy Crockett at the Alamo" (February 23, 1955). Only one character was a constant in addition to Fess Parker's portrayal of Crockett: Hollywood veteran and former song-and-dance man Buddy Ebsen, who appeared as his sidekick, Georgie Russell.

With Crockett's death at the Alamo, the series had seemingly run its course (since even legends don't return from the grave), but the public's demand for more episodes resulted in a few more slightly inferior episodes being produced. Crockett's chief antagonist in these episodes was Mike Fink (Jeff York), the riverman's answer to Paul Bunyan. All of these events supposedly took place earlier in Crockett's life.

While the extra episodes had no basis in fact, the others did and this may have helped account for the Crockett craze. Heroes were needed, and here was one who fought the Indians alongside Andrew Jackson, served in Congress, and was supposedly the last man left alive at the Alamo when it fell to the Mexican forces led by General Santa Ana on March 6, 1836.

Sometimes even the most unglamorous truth can be glamorized and sanitized. The real Davy Crockett did fight in the Creek Wars with Andrew Jackson, he did serve in Congress (although, being semiliterate, it's highly unlikely he was responsible for much legislation during his one term in Washington), and he did die at the Alamo. Legend has it, however, that Crockett did not go down fighting; he, along with a black slave and a Mexican woman, surrendered, and Crockett alone of the three survivors was executed by a firing squad. Or so one legend goes. If that particular version is true — and it seems to be the one repeated most often — Crockett was indeed the last defender of the Alamo to die, although not as heroically as depicted.

Crockett wasn't the only Western series produced by Disney, as Davy begat Andy Burnett, another frontiersman (see "The Saga of Andy Burnette"); Elfego Baca ("The Nine Lives of Elfego Baca"); Texas John Slaughter (his series bore the same name); Revolutionary War hero Francis Marion ("The Swamp Fox"); and, of course, Zorro, the only Disney hero ever to have his own weekly series.

Except for Zorro, none of the Disney heroes lasted a full season, but no doubt would have had they been presented with the opportunity. However, there is no denying they were an integral part of television's Western lore. It's probably just as well none of them did last a full season; there was a certain mystique about something that was

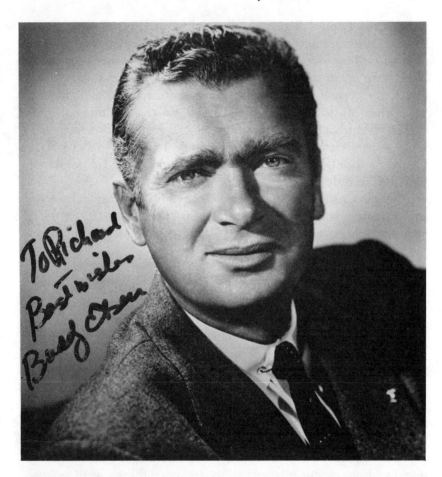

Although he is equally remembered as Davy Crockett's sidekick Georgie Russell or as Jed Clampett on the long-running situation comedy "The Beverly Hillbillies," Buddy Ebsen started out his career as a song-and-dance man in vaudeville. That may be why, if you wrote and asked for a picture, you received one of him in a suit and tie — but true fans of the genre knew that under that contemporary facade beats the heart of a frontiersman.

only on a few times, and a series might have resulted in overkill, with the memories being less fond than they are.

There had been Westerns, cowboys and Indians, gunfighters, and so on long before Disney presented the Crockett series. However, to old Davy must go the full credit for opening the floodgates.

Recorded Theme Music: "The Ballad of Davy Crockett," Bill Hayes, Columbia Records. "The Ballad of Davy Crockett," Tennessee

Ernie Ford, Capitol Records. "The Ballad of Davy Crockett," Fess Parker, Columbia Records. Of the three, Ford's version was the most popular, selling several million copies. The version by "Days of Our Lives" soap opera star Hayes is probably the most scarce, but next to Ford's, the version in most demand by record collectors is Parker's.

Other Music of Interest: "Farewell (to the Mountains)," Fess Parker, Columbia Records (this is the song Crockett/Parker sang on TV while at the Alamo the night of March 5, 1836), "Old Betsy (Davy Crockett's Rifle)," and the Sons of the Pioneers, RCA Children's Bluebird Records.

All the Crockett adventures were edited for theatrical release into approximately 90 minute movies (for the European market) and are now available on video-cassette.

# The Adventures of Jim Bowie
### *ABC, September 1956–August 1958*

This series was set in the Louisiana Territory during the early 1830s, a few years before Bowie was to go to Texas, where he later died at the Alamo. Scott Forbes portrayed a rather dashing Bowie in much the same manner that Fess Parker portrayed Davy Crockett.

The show was based quite loosely on the life of the real Bowie. Not coincidentally, the series aired after Bowie became a 1950s legend following the "Davy Crockett" episodes on the Walt Disney series.

Bowie's life — that of a wealthy young adventurer who would occasionally drop by his plantation to see how things were going — intertwined with other legends of the time, both real and fictitious, such as Andrew Jackson, Sam Houston, his good friend and naturalist painter John James Audubon (Robert Cornthwaite), the pirate Jean Lafitte, Johnny Appleseed, and, of course, Crockett. The appearance of the latter gave rise to one of the series' sillier episodes in which the Louisiana-based Bowie ran for Congress against the Tennessee-based Crockett — but remember Crockett-mania was at its height at that time, and it was perfectly acceptable to take a few liberties with historical fact. Rarely on the series was a shot fired in anger, since Bowie used his famous namesake knife (which had, in reality, been designed by his brother) while others used guns. In addition to Forbes and Cornthwaite, the series' other continuing character was Rezin Bowie, Jim's brother, played by Peter Hanson.

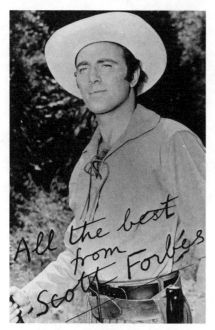 

Scott Forbes, whose sole involvement with television was the lead role in "The Adventures of Jim Bowie" on ABC from 1956 to 1958.

Recorded Theme Music: "Jim Bowie," the Prairie Chiefs, RCA Children's Bluebird Records.

# The Adventures of Kit Carson
*Syndicated*

Bill Williams had one of those faces you immediately recognized when you saw him. Perhaps his name was even familiar, since it seemed as though he popped up on literally every other program during the 1950s and 1960s. Like so many others, he received his opportunity to play cowboy and ride the range in a series which had about as much to do with the exploits of the famed frontiersman as did those of the Man from Glad. The real Kit Carson roamed the frontier prior to 1850 and was a member of the famed Fremont Expedition, which traversed such Western states as Wyoming and Colorado before winding up in California. In this series, however, he was just another cowboy, although he did wear buckskins to present a minor brush with reality.

For frontiersman authenticity, Davy Crockett, Andy Burnette, and Daniel Boone were considerably more accurate. Don Diamond appeared as Carson's Mexican sidekick, El Toro.

## The Adventures of Rin Tin Tin
### ABC, October 1954–August 1959

This series was kids' stuff, pure and simple. After all, how much believability could you attach to the fact that a German Shepherd played a major part in saving the Old West, not to mention making it safe?

By the time the series aired, Rin Tin Tin was already on the road to becoming an American legend, the first dog with that name having appeared in the movies in 1922.

Along with Lee Aaker as Rusty, James Brown as Lt. Rip Masters, Joe Sawyer as Sgt. Biff O'Hara, and Rand Brooks as Cpl. Boone, Rin Tin Tin (or Rinty as he was called) lived at Fort Apache in the Arizona Territory. He had been found, along with Rusty, following an Indian raid that left the boy an orphan. Naturally, both were found by the cavalry and moved into the fort, becoming a couple of the boys, with Rusty even having his own miniature army uniform.

Appearing in the series apparently took its toll on the famed canine, as no fewer than three dogs were utilized during the series' five-year run.

## The Alaskans
### ABC, October 1959–September 1960

Before he went on to greater fame by portraying Agent 007, James Bond, Roger Moore served time in a number of television series. None proved to be highly successful, and some he would probably just as soon forget. *The Alaskans* is no doubt one of the latter series. Throughout all Moore's series, though, there was one common denominator: he always wound up portraying a suave, debonair type. This one—his first starring role—was no exception.

Silky Harris (Moore) and his companions Reno McKee (Jeff York), Nifty Cronin (Ray Danton), and Rocky Shaw (Dorothy Provine), set out for Skagway, Alaska in the 1890s to seek their fortunes. Not being overly enamored of the work ethic, they soon attempted to make those fortunes in places other than the gold fields. Rocky went to work for the less-than-straightforward Nifty, singing in his saloon, while Silky and Reno would rely upon Silky's charm to con their victims.

A month after this series bit the dust, Provine wound up in a somewhat similar role as Pinky Pinkham in the dramatic series "The Roaring Twenties," which at least lasted two years, but marked the end of her involvement with series television. It was to be a few years yet— not to mention several series—before Moore found lasting fame as James Bond.

# Alias Smith and Jones
## ABC, January 1971–January 1973

This series attempted to answer two questions. First, what do you, a TV executive, do when a hit movie like *Butch Cassidy and the Sundance Kid,* which starred Paul Newman and Robert Redford, comes along? The answer, of course, is you make an obvious rip-off "ABC Movie of the Week," and when it garners sufficiently high ratings, you make it a series. In other words, you continue an old standard TV practice.

The other question isn't so simple to answer, though. What do you do when one of your stars commits suicide midway through the first season? Do you run the remaining episodes that have already been filmed and let your stars ride off into the sunset, or do you recast the part and hope that no one will notice the difference? ABC chose to opt for the latter, and while the viewers obviously noticed that Roger Davis was not Pete Duel (Hannibal Heyes, aka Joshua Smith) the change apparently had little effect on the show's ratings, as it continued for another year. Davis was no stranger to the series' viewers, since he had been doing the opening narration, so viewers were at least accustomed to his voice, if not his face.

Duel, then Davis, were Heyes, with Ben Murphy his sidekick "Kid" Curry (aka Thaddeus Jones), two lovable outlaws straight out of the Butch Cassidy and Sundance Kid mold who were attempting to go straight. The pair had been promised a pardon by the governor if they could keep themselves out of trouble for a year, something which wasn't easy to do considering that they were still wanted desperadoes who kept running into either bounty hunters or old outlaw friends who wanted them to join in on some escapade which, if not illegal, was borderline. When they finally hung up their spurs and rode off into the sunset, they still hadn't received their pardon, but if they had would this somewhat tongue-in-cheek oater have been any better?

In an attempt to boost ratings, in late 1971 Sally Field was added in a sporadic but continuing role as Clementine Hale. While many still remember her for her role in one of the sillier situation comedies of all time, "The Flying Nun," the Hale role gave her an opportunity to start shedding that less-than-welcome association. It was to be a few years, however, before she was finally able to shake the image completely and gain acceptance as a serious actress.

# The Americans
## NBC, January 1961–September 1961

In the early 1960s, America was marking the one hundredth anniversary of the Civil War. What better way to commemorate the occasion than with a TV series? But, while there may have been a fascination with the War Between the States, there was little fascination with this series featuring the adventures and exploits of two brothers, Ben (Darryl Hickman, the brother of "Dobie Gillis" star Dwayne Hickman) and Jeff Canfield (Dick Davalos), one of whom wore blue while the other wore grey.

Growing up in Harper's Ferry, Virginia, the site of abolitionist John Brown's raid, the two were faced with the decision of whether to fight when Virginia seceded from the Union in 1861. Jeff, the younger of the pair, decided to fight for the Confederacy. Ben enlisted in the Union Army following a disastrous fire which killed their father in the opening episode. Each brother was then featured on an alternating basis, with Ben fighting for the Union and Jeff serving in the Virginia Military with the Confederate forces.

As the year wound down, the series did as well, and the war ended for the Canfield brothers before a full year had passed.

# Annie Oakley
## Syndicated

In a first for television Westerns, Gail Davis was the heroine in a series that was strictly for the younger set. Brad Johnson appeared as

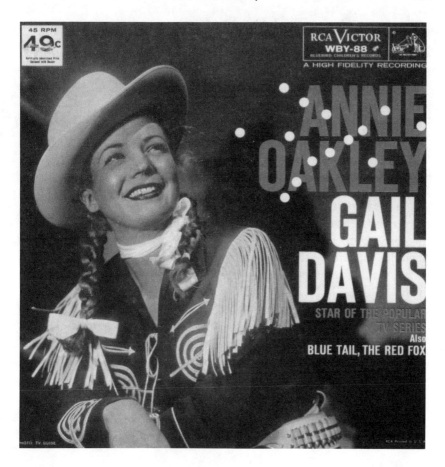

"Annie Oakley" was one of the first series of any kind to have a female in the starring role and was one of the few Westerns ever to have a female lead. Davis was discovered by Gene Autry while in college in Texas, and the syndicated series starring her was, naturally, a Gene Autry production. Any resemblance between Davis and the real Annie Oakley is purely coincidental.

Sheriff Lofty Craig and Jimmy Hoskins was Annie's kid brother Tag, which may have stood for Tagalong, since it seemed he was always getting in the way and was where he wasn't supposed to be. While there was a real Annie Oakley, it's highly unlikely she ever looked as good as Davis or performed any of the feats she did on the series.

Recorded Theme Music: "Annie Oakley," Gail Davis, RCA Children's Bluebird Records.

# The Barbary Coast
*ABC, September 1975–January 1976*

By the time this series hit the air, Westerns were rapidly becoming an endangered species. This show was one of the last efforts by any of the networks to keep the Old West alive in one form or another.

Between his appearances in two highly successful series—the legendary "Star Trek" on which he portrayed Captain James T. Kirk, commander of the Starship *Enterprise*, and "T.J. Hooker," on which he appeared as the police sergeant of the same name, William Shatner put in a few months' television service as Jeff Cable, a special agent and master of disguise who was working for the governor of California. His mission: not to seek out strange new worlds and make contact where possible, but to gather as much information as possible on the widespread criminal element in San Francisco's Barbary Coast district in the 1870s.

Veteran Western actor Doug McClure was Cash Conover, the owner of the Golden Gate Casino and Cable's ally. Richard Kiel, who is probably best remembered for his role of Jaws in the James Bond movie *Moonraker*, appeared as Moose Moran.

# Bat Masterson
*ABC, October 1958–September 1961*

While television audiences probably couldn't (or wouldn't) have accepted a series featuring the exploits, or lack thereof, of the real William Bartley "Bat" Masterson as a New York sportswriter in his later years, for three years they did accept Gene Barry's portrayal of his earlier life in the Old West as that of a dapper, well-educated, debonair, smooth-talking professional gambler, lawman, scout and Indian fighter, the type of role which Barry made a career out of portraying. With the exception of a year when he played Eve Arden's love interest, Gene Talbot, in "Our Miss Brooks," all of Barry's roles were of this kind. In later years, he was to move on to play the aristocratic cop Amos Burke in the series of the same name and the distinguished head of a magazine publishing empire in "The Name of the Game."

Roaming throughout the West and Southwest, Masterson, with

his derby hat and cane, was portrayed as one who preferred to talk his adversaries out of a gunfight if possible, resorting to violence only when he was unable to disarm them with words or with his cane. Masterson was a close friend of Wyatt Earp, and this friendship could have provided material for a number of episodes, but the friendship was only alluded to and no one ever appeared portraying the other Western legend, possibly because of the presence of Hugh O'Brian's Earp series on the same network during the same years (the networks hadn't yet begun the practice of having the stars of one series appear on another series).

# The Big Valley
### ABC, September 1965–May 1969

If you took the Cartwrights off the Ponderosa, moved them to California's San Joaquin Valley, replaced Lorne Greene with veteran actress Barbara Stanwyck, and added a daughter, you would basically have "The Big Valley."

If nothing else, though, the series introduced Lee Majors (Heath Barkley) and Linda Evans (Audra Barkley) to the American viewing public, and any program which gave us Linda Evans can't be all bad. Others appearing in the series were Stanwyck (Victoria Barkley), former "Maverick" co-star Richard Long (Jarrod Barkley), Peter Breck (Nick Barkley), and Silas, the butler (Napoleon Whiting).

On the Barkley's ranch and in the nearby environs in the 1870s, Stanwyck, like her male counterpart on the Ponderosa, kept her eye on things with the help of her sons: Jarrod, a lawyer, and Nick and Heath, who spent their time running the ranching end of the family's business and, of course, fighting the lawless elements with which the family came into frequent contact. Meanwhile, Audra was always present to provide romantic interludes for any strangers passing through the area (they always were).

While the whole family were Barkleys, one son, Heath, was the illegitimate son of Victoria's late husband Tom, who obviously didn't spend all his time on the ranch. Heath's introduction into the series and his subsequent acceptance by the Barkley clan provided the series with material for several of the earlier episodes.

Majors, who was to later become a notable star with several successful series, had no previous acting experience, and the role of

Heath was the first he auditioned for. Evans went on to bigger and better things as well, becoming one of television's biggest stars in the prime-time soap opera "Dynasty."

# Black Saddle
*NBC, January 1959–September 1959*
*ABC, October 1959–September 1960*

For one year, Clay Culhane (Peter Breck) rode the airwaves at NBC and for another at ABC, always followed by United States Marshall Gib Scott (Russell Johnson) who felt the former gunslinger hadn't really traded in his guns for law books and thus had a compulsion to keep his eye on Culhane to insure that he walked the straight-and-narrow path. And that was the basic premise of the show: Former gunslinger travels around the New Mexico Territory in post–Civil War era, helping those who needed the aid and assistance of a lawyer.

Johnson probably wished he had a lawyer in later years to get him out of his role when he appeared as the Professor on one of television's more ridiculous situation comedies, "Gilligan's Island." But, it was better than standing in the unemployment line.

# Bonanza
*NBC, September 1959–January 1973*

For no less than 14 years, in television's second-longest–running Western, the Cartwrights of Virginia City, Nevada, offered viewers a steady diet of comedy, tragedy and pathos, not to mention good old Western action. Obviously, the formula and the interaction between the characters were successful.

Led by their patriarch, Ben Cartwright (Lorne Greene), and living on the 1000-square-mile Ponderosa ranch during the Civil War years, the clan consisted of Adam (Pernell Roberts), Hoss (Dan Blocker), and Little Joe (Michael Landon). All were half-brothers, each born to one of Ben's successive wives, none of whom survived the rigors of the Old West before Ben had made his fortune. His three marriages did provide material for flashback episodes periodically during the show's run.

Of the three sons, only Little Joe was still around at the conclusion of the series' run on January 16, 1973. Roberts was the first to leave

**Although he is probably remembered more for his role as Nick Barkley on "The Big Valley," which ran for four years, for two years Peter Breck appeared as Clay Culhane on "Black Saddle."**

following the 1965 season, supposedly because he was tired of the weekly grind, although his next try at series television, "Trapper John, M.D.," was a CBS Sunday night staple for over five years. Blocker, meanwhile, died unexpectedly prior to the start of the 1972–73 season.

One non–family member, the Chinese cook Hop Sing (Victor Sen Yung), was also with the program from its beginning on September 12, 1959. David Canary portrayed the ranch hand Candy from 1967 to

1970 and again in 1972–73, making him the only other cast member of any duration. Three others, Dusty Rhoades (Lou Frizzell), Jamie Hunter (Mitch Vogel), and Griff King (Tim Matheson) were also principal characters in the early 1970s (Matheson attempted to fill the void left by Blocker's untimely death). Matheson, though, was destined for bigger things, showing up as one of the stars of the successful hit movie *National Lampoon's Animal House* a few years later.

The first Western to be televised in color, "Bonanza" made its first appearance on a Saturday night, moving to Sunday two years later, remaining there until moving into a Tuesday night time slot for its final season. For most of the 1960s, it was one of the highest-rated programs on television, being number one from 1964 to 1967, ironically the same three-year period when "Gunsmoke" fell out of the top 20.

A nontraditional Western in the sense that it relied more on the interplay and personal relationships of the characters than on gunslinging action, the show generally centered around one particular family member each week with the others playing, in effect, supporting roles. The adventures and misadventures of the family formed the basis for most of the series' stories.

The Canadian-born Greene made a career out of playing father-figures, appearing in a similar role in the short-lived science fiction series "Battlestar Galactica," where he was Commander Adama from 1978 to 1979. After "Bonanza" was cancelled, he was a father-figure cop in the detective drama "Griff" in 1973–74.

Landon, whose initial television appearance was on "The Adventures of Jim Bowie" in 1956, also took a turn at playing a father-figure in the wholesome, squeaky-clean drama series "Little House on the Prairie" which premiered on NBC in September 1974, and seemingly ran forever. He currently stars in another wholesome series, "Highway to Heaven," also on NBC.

Recorded Theme Music: Original instrumental version, "Bonanza," Al Caiola, United Artists Records. Although no vocal version was ever heard on television, Johnny Cash recorded one for Columbia Records.

# Boots and Saddles
*Syndicated*

Set in the Arizona Territory in the 1870s, this story of the Fifth Cavalry stationed at Fort Lowell first hit the small screen in 1958. Jack

Pickard starred as Shank Adams, with Michael Hinn appearing as Luke Cummings, the faithful (and no doubt grizzled) Indian scout.

# Branded
### NBC, January 1965–September 1966

Following the demise of "The Rifleman" in 1963, Chuck Connors donned a suit and tie and attempted to inject believability into his role as a lawyer in the short-lived series "Arrest and Trial." But it was obvious he was just an old cowboy, and he wound up back on the range again in 1965 as Jason McCord, a West Point graduate with a successful army career who had risen to the rank of captain before being drummed out of the service, unjustly accused of being a coward. As the theme song said, "All but one man died there at Bitter Creek. . ." and, of course, McCord was that man. Judging from the number of people with whom McCord came in contact who had relatives at the massacre, the death toll must have been in the thousands.

As he travelled around the West in the 1880s, he attempted to obtain proof he was just as brave as the next man, encountering just as many who believed him a coward as those who didn't. Among those who obviously believed him to be innocent was the president of the United States, who called upon him for aid and assistance on several occasions. Why he was never pardoned and his rank restored by the president was a mystery, although it would have killed off the idea behind the series.

In his travels, McCord could be counted upon to run across some of the more famous Americans of that period, including the actor Edwin Booth, for whom he served as a bodyguard on one episode. Booth, naturally, had his own problems, being the brother of John Wilkes Booth, who assassinated Abraham Lincoln.

# Brave Eagle
### CBS, September 1955–June 1956

This was possibly a case of a series being a few years ahead of its time since it presented the encroachment of the white man onto the Indian's lands from the Indian's point of view. In 1955–56, there were the Bad Guys: Indians, Mexicans, gunslingers; and then there were the Good Guys: cattle ranchers, frontiersmen, homesteaders, and the U.S. Cavalry. Indians—other than Cochise in "Broken Arrow" and Tonto on "The Lone Ranger" and perhaps one or two others—were not the Good Guys and weren't usually presented in that light until the 1960s, when "civil rights" became a household phrase.

Nevertheless, Brave Eagle (Keith Larsen), his foster son Keena (Keena Nomkeena), Morning Star (Kim Winona), an Indian girl with whom he was loosely romantically linked, and Smokey Joe (Bert Wheeler), an old halfbreed who could be counted upon to pass along bits of wisdom, weekly fought other Indians, nature, and of course, the white man who was coming closer and closer to his land.

# Broken Arrow
*ABC, September 1956–September 1958*

If you could accept the premise that Cochise, the most powerful chief of the Chiracahua Apaches, was really a super-nice guy deep down inside, you could accept this series, which presented Michael Ansara as Cochise, a slightly misunderstood chief who actually had a heart of gold and wouldn't harm a fly. And if you could accept that, you could no doubt accept the premise that Indian agent Tom Jeffords (John Lupton) was his blood brother and that together the two of them spent their time fighting off renegades from the reservation and desperadoes who were out to prey upon the Indians.

If you knew your history, you knew the whole thing was a silly fabrication, but it still proved to be somewhat interesting and entertaining. To make Cochise appear even tamer, in the opening episode when peace negotiations were underway, one obstinate and hot-blooded brave announced he couldn't live in peace with the white man on their terms; he was going to adopt the name given him by the Mexicans as a form of protest, and in effect he was no longer an Apache. That name? Geronimo, which proves that perhaps Cochise wasn't as bad as some of the others.

The series was based on the Elliott Arnold novel of the same name, which had been made into a movie in 1950.

Recorded Theme Music: "Broken Arrow," the Prairie Chiefs, RCA Children's Bluebird Records.

*Top:* In "Broken Arrow," John Lupton (*left*) was Indian agent Tom Jeffords, who was also the blood brother of Cochise (Michael Ansara, *right*). The series was one of the first to present an Indian in a favorable light rather than portraying them all as cold, emotionless savages. *Bottom*: While he may look like an Indian and usually wound up playing one, Michael Ansara is, in fact, Lebanese. From 1956 to 1958, he portrayed the legendary Apache Indian chief, Cochise, in "Broken Arrow."

From 1958 to 1962, Ty Hardin was Bronco Layne in "Bronco," one of the series which, along with "Sugarfoot," was designed to take the place of Clint Walker's "Cheyenne." In time, "Bronco" was part of a rotating anthology, all under the "Cheyenne" banner.

# Bronco
### ABC, September 1958–August 1962

For four years Ty Hardin apppeared as Bronco Layne, an ex–Confederate Army captain who roamed the Wild West occasionally. Unlike most cowboys, he didn't roam every week, roaming instead every other week, if he roamed at all. Confused? The story of Bronco Layne tends to be one of confusion, but the first thing to remember is that the series came from Warner Brothers.

Had Clint Walker never quit his series, "Cheyenne," in 1958, Bronco might never have come into being. As a matter of fact, "Cheyenne" continued under its original banner after Walker's departure, but the show was really about Bronco. Then in 1959, Walker returned to "Cheyenne," and "Bronco" became a separate series, alternating with Will Hutchins' "Sugarfoot" for two years. In 1960, it returned under the "Cheyenne" title in a rotating anthology along with "Sugarfoot." After Hutchins' series bit the dust in 1961, "Bronco" and "Cheyenne" alternated until Bronco Layne also rode off into the sunset, no doubt still trying to figure out whether he was Bronco or Cheyenne or someone else.

# Buckskin
## *NBC, July 1958–September 1959*

Not much happened in the town of Buckskin, Montana, in 1880, but the writers of this series managed to think up enough tales involving the adventures and misadventures of ten-year-old Jody O'Connell (Tommy Nolan) to keep it on the air for a year. Nolan lived in his mother's boardinghouse, the center of all activity in Buckskin, which gives some idea as to how exciting things were in that part of Montana. Sallie Brophy played his mother, Mrs. Annie O'Connell, and Michael Road was the obligatory marshal, Tom Sellers. Road was to later move into the twentieth century and beyond, first playing police lieutenant Joe Switolski in "The Roaring Twenties" and then providing the voice of Race Bannon on the cartoon series "Johnny Quest."

# Buffalo Bill, Jr.
## *Syndicated*

As anyone who knows anything at all about the Old West can readily attest, there was no real Buffalo Bill, Jr. There *was* a real Buffalo Bill (Cody), and why he was never the subject of a series is a good question, since everyone else who ever rode the range had a series named after him. Regardless, the name was recognizable and therefore exploitable. That the series had absolutely no connection with Buffalo Bill was beside the point.

Dick Jones, a veteran of syndicated Westerns, starred as a quick-on-the-draw orphan who found a home as the adopted son of a good-hearted judge.

# The Californians
## *NBC, September 1957–August 1959*

As originally conceived and presented, the series was to be the story of Dion Patrick (Adam Kennedy), who had been drawn to San

*Left:* When it started out in 1957, "The Californians" was supposed to center around the adventures of Dion Patrick (Adam Kennedy) in San Francisco at the height of the California Gold Rush. While Kennedy soon found himself ousted by veteran actor Richard Coogan, he was with the series long enough to have publicity photos made. *Right:* The 6-foot, 6-inch Clint Walker surely wasn't a favorite of Warner Brothers management, even though "Cheyenne" ran for eight years. His contract dispute with the studio in 1958 resulted in the series continuing with Ty Hardin as Bronco Layne until the dispute could be settled and Walker coaxed back in front of the cameras. His only other try at series television, "Kodiak," was nowhere near as successful, lasting only five weeks in 1974.

Francisco at the height of the California Gold Rush and who wound up working as a crusading newspaper reporter for Sam Brennan (Herbert Rudley). In an attempt to help keep law and order in the City by the Bay, he joined the vigilantes who had been organized by Jack McGivern (Sean McClory). At that time, the vigilantes represented the only law enforcement agency in town and were supposedly better than nothing.

By the middle of the first season, though, Richard Coogan, who had achieved some sort of notoriety by being the original Captain

Video in 1949–50 arrived on the scene as Matthew Wayne and soon found himself elected sheriff, a fact which meant that vigilantes Patrick and McGivern were sent sailing on a slow boat to China.

In the series' second season, Wayne was elevated to city marshal with a reorganized 50-man police force, which helped him maintain law and order in a town experiencing growing pains. Able to mingle with the best of San Francisco society, yet flexible enough to talk with the roughest of prospectors, Wayne also acquired the mandatory love interest in Wilma Fansler (Carole Mathews), who ran the obligatory gambling house. Replacing Patrick as Wayne's friend was Jeremy Pitt (Arthur Fleming), an attorney who proved to be Wayne's adversary at times.

# Cheyenne
### ABC, September 1955–September 1963

Part of Warner Brothers Studios' first foray into television programming, "Cheyenne" was basically a one-man show, with 6-foot, 6-inch Clint Walker portraying Cheyenne Bodie, a drifter throughout the West in the days following the Civil War. During the first season he had a sidekick, Smitty, played by L.Q. Jones, who quickly rode off into the sunset when it became apparent Walker didn't need any help. Basically, the show was typical Western fare, with plenty of bad guys, good guys, gunfights, and Indians. That was pretty tame stuff compared to the fighting that was going on between Walker and the studio.

Following a contract dispute with the studio in 1958, Walker walked, but the studio, undeterred, continued the series under the "Cheyenne" banner with Ty Hardin appearing as Bronco Layne. Coming to a somewhat satisfactory agreement with the studio, Walker returned in early 1959 while Hardin continued in his own series, "Bronco."

During its initial run, "Cheyenne" was seen as one-third of 'Warner Brothers Presents," alternating with the dramatic anthology series "Conflict" in 1956–57 and with Will Hutchins in "Sugarfoot" from 1957 to 1959. By 1959–60, the series was alternating with "Shirley Temple's Storybook," remaining in the Top 20 Nielsen ratings where it had been during most of its run, reaching a high of thirteenth in 1957–58. In 1960–61, nearing the end of the trail, it became "The

Cheyenne Show," in which our old friend Bronco appeared once again on a rotating basis along with "Sugarfoot," although Walker appeared in a majority of the shows.

The following year it was only "Bronco" and "Cheyenne," with the last three months of the series being "Cheyenne" reruns.

After "Cheyenne" bit the dust, Walker didn't give series television a try again until 1974 when he played a member of the Alaska State Patrol in "Kodiak." A series with nowhere near the staying power of "Cheyenne," it lasted a total of five weeks. In recent years, Walker has become a spokesman for Kal Kan Dog Food.

Recorded Theme Music: As in the case of so many programs, there was no vocal version of the theme heard. However, a vocal rendition was recorded by the Sons of the Pioneers on RCA Children's Bluebird Records.

# Cimarron City
### NBC, October 1958–September 1959

Other than "Bonanza," the late Dan Blocker appeared in only one series on a continuing basis and this was it. Blocker played Tiny Budinger, a local citizen who frequently wound up helping out the marshal. Unfortunately for Blocker, the series starred veteran actor George Montgomery in his sole try at series television, and top billing went to Montgomery, not Blocker. However, as soon as this series bit the dust, which wasn't too long, Blocker moved on to the Ponderosa to become Hoss Cartwright, and the rest is television history.

Cimarron City, Oklahoma, in the 1890s was a booming metropolitan area (for its time) whose citizenry had dreams of becoming residents of the state capital without moving to Oklahoma City. Matthew Rockford (Montgomery) was mayor and the obligatory cattle rancher who narrated the show detailing what had happened to him in his younger days. Beth Purcell (Audrey Totter) was the owner of the equally obligatory boardinghouse, and Lane Temple (John Smith) was the sheriff. Naturally, most of the action in the series centered around the adventures of this dynamic threesome.

Also appearing were Stuart Randall as Art Sampson, Addison Richards as Martin Kingsley, Fred Sherman as Burt Purdy, Claire Carleton as Alice Purdy, George Dunn as Jesse Williams, Pete Dunn as Dody Hammer, Tom Fadden as Silas Perry, and Wally Brown as Jed Fame.

## Cimarron Strip
### CBS, September 1967–September 1968

There must be something about the word "Cimarron" when it's in a series title since the only two television series in history with that word in the title managed to last just a year apiece.

In the early 1880s — the series supposedly began in 1882, according to one episode — the 10 million–acre area in the Cherokee Outlet, that portion of Oklahoma which constitutes the state's panhandle, was known as the Cimarron Strip, and it fell to 35-year-old Marshal Jim Crown (Stuart Whitman) to keep law and order in the area. This was Whitman's sole attempt at a regular role in series television, although he was on seemingly every other program in guest roles.

A former hell-raiser of sorts who elected to put on a badge and calm down, he was apparently expected to perform this peacekeeping task by himself, since he was given no deputies. As a result, he often found himself calling upon Francis Wilde (Randy Boone), a young photographer and would-be writer, along with the Scotsman known as MacGregor (Percy Herbert), for aid and assistance. Eighteen-year-old Dulcy Coopersmith (Jill Townsend) ran the Wayfarers Inn and was the other series regular. It was obvious she had her eyes on Crown, but it was equally obvious Crown was a confirmed bachelor and thought of her more as a younger sister.

A somewhat underrated series, it was another 90-minute epic.

## The Cisco Kid
### Syndicated

If the word "gay" had meant in the 1950s what it means today, you might have been safe in referring to Cisco and his sidekick Pancho as gay caballeros. For some reason, you just had to wonder about these two. Duncan Renaldo was Cisco and Leo Carillo was Pancho, and while ethnic types weren't exactly hot items, this pair of Mexican do-gooders rode the range for a number of years.

Most episodes usually ended with the pair sharing a joke, and "Oh, Cisco," "Oh, Pancho," became the standard sign-off

As originally conceived and carried on radio in 1942, the duo was promoted as a pair of outlaws who, like Robin Hood, took from the rich and greedy and gave to the poor. After that initial foray, the series disappeared until 1946, at which time all references to their outlaw nature were gone. Now they were two Mexican adventurers, with Cisco, not to mention Pancho, inevitably triumphing over evil. And, as it would be on television, it was always "Oh, Cisco," and "Oh, Pancho," with the pair spurring on their horses, Diablo and Loco, as they rode off to new adventures.

Strictly for the kids, the series was one of the longest-lasting syndicated series to be filmed.

# Colgate Western Theatre
### NBC, July 1959–September 1959

For a little over two months during the summer of 1959, in case you missed them the first time around or wanted to see them again, you were afforded the opportunity of viewing reruns of selected Westerns originally shown on the "G.E. Theatre" and "Schlitz Playhouse."

# Colt .45
### ABC, October 1957–September 1960

Wayde Preston portrayed Christopher Colt. Wayde Preston was also under contract to Warner Brothers, which produced this series along with a myriad of others, and therein lies an oft-told story. Like the other Warner Brothers malcontents, Preston walked out during the series run, which led to the network being forced to air a number of repeat episodes along with the original ones it had remaining until, in 1959, Preston found himself replaced by Donald May in the role of Sam Colt, Jr. Although Preston did eventually come to make his peace with the studio, May had by that time taken over as the lead character in the series—but it was actually a moot point since the show was soon cancelled.

Essentially, the series was about a government undercover agent,

The theme song said Christopher Colt (Wayde Preston) was "a lightnin' bolt when he drew that Colt .45," and he left the series just about that fast in one of the numerous contract disputes the stars of Warner Brothers' series seemed to have with the studio. Preston was able to make peace, but by that time the series had been cancelled, so it made little or no difference.

first Preston, then May, who was posing as a gun salesman for, you guessed it, the Colt Firearms Company. Since most of the episodes involved tracking down dangerous and nefarious outlaws, there were a great many opportunities presented to use the faithful Colt .45. When May joined the series, it was explained that he was Christopher Colt's cousin and he just happened to be a government agent as well.

# Cowboy in Africa
*ABC, September 1967–September 1968*

This may or may not have been a Western in the true sense of the word, depending upon your point of view, but despite the locale, it had most of the essential ingredients. So for the sake of argument, let's call it a Western, albeit a different type of one. And while it may have been set on the Dark Continent, most of the action really took place in the Africa, U.S.A., park in southern California. Only the backgrounds were authentically African.

Definitely a contemporary series, it tended to present a welcome relief to those who were tired of over a decade of Indians fighting the U.S. Cavalry. Chuck Connors was world champion rodeo cowboy Jim Sinclair who had been hired to bring modern ranching methods to the Kenyan game preserve of Wing Commander Howard Hayes (Ronald Howard), an English landowner. Assisting Sinclair in fighting off the elephants were his Navajo blood brother (well, there had to be an Indian in there someplace), John Henry (Tom Nardini), and an orphaned ten-year-old Kikuyu native boy, Samson (Gerald Edwards).

The series was more or less based upon Ivan Tors' film *Africa— Texas Style.*

# Cowboy Theatre
*NBC, June 1957–September 1957*

Although it began on Saturday afternoons in 1956, this less-than-original series made its prime-time debut about ten months later and died shortly thereafter. Hosted by Monty Hall, who was destined to go down in television history as the host of the inane game show "Let's Make a Deal," it consisted solely of reedited feature films produced by Columbia Pictures in the 1930s and 1940s.

# The Cowboys
*ABC, February 1974–August 1974*

Based somewhat loosely on the movie of the same name starring John Wayne, which was in turn based on the novel by William Dale

Jennings, this series presented (for a short period of time) the trials and tribulations of seven young boys, aged 9 to 14, who were growing up on a ranch in the New Mexico Territory during the 1870s. Moses Gunn, who was to turn up on the situation comedy "Good Times" in 1977, was foreman Jebediah Nightlinger. The ranch's owner, the widowed Mrs. Annie Anderson (Diana Douglas), and veteran character actor Jim Davis as Marshal Bill Winter were the only adults besides Gunn appearing on a regular basis. Davis, of course, is best remembered for his role as Jock Ewing in the prime-time soap opera "Dallas." The boys were: Cimarron (A. Martinez), Slim (Robert Carradine), Jimmy (Sean Kelly), Homer (Kerry MacLane), Steve (Clint Howard), Hardy (Mitch Brown), and Weedy (Clay O'Brien). Four of them—Martinez, Carradine, Kelly, and O'Brien—also appeared in the movie.

# Custer
### ABC, September 1967–December 1967

Was George Armstrong Custer a true Western hero or an egocentric glory hunter who had his eyes on the presidency? It's a question that historians have been debating for years. If you chose to believe this series, however, there was no doubt that the somewhat unconventional general was a hero in the truest sense of the word, not to mention that his hair (shoulder-length in real life) was short and neatly cut.

In just four short months, Wayne Maunder as Custer lost his Civil War rank of brevet major general, was shipped to Fort Hayes, Kansas, to take command of the Seventh Cavalry, managed to organize a motley crew of misfit soldiers into an extremely efficient fighting force, and protected the settlers. In actuality, this feat took a little over six years between 1868 and 1874, with the Seventh moving into the Sioux Territory near the Little Big Horn in 1875, the year before the famous battle that took the life of Custer along with the rest of his troops.

Custer was aided by his faithful companion and scout, California Joe Milner (Slim Pickens), Capt. Miles Keogh (Grant Woods), and Sgt. James Bustard (Peter Palmer). In addition to his somewhat continuing conflict with Crazy Horse (Michael Dante), Custer was often at odds with the commander of Fort Hayes, Brig. Gen. Alfred Terry (Robert F. Simon).

# The Dakotas
*ABC, January 1963–September 1963*

Marshal Frank Ragan (Larry Ward) and his three deputies, J.D. Smith (Jack Elam), Del Stark (Chad Everett), and Vance Porter (Mike Greene), attempted to maintain law and order in the Black Hills and Badlands of the Dakota Territory, but not for long. In a few years, Everett was to move on to bigger and better things, portraying Dr. Joe Gannon on the long-running (1969–76) "Medical Center" on CBS.


# Daniel Boone
*NBC, September 1964–August 1970*

This show held down the Thursday evening time slot from 7:30 to 8:30 throughout its entire six-year run. NBC's reasoning behind the show must have been, "If Fess Parker was believable as Davy Crockett, let's put him back in buckskins, call him Daniel Boone and see what happens." Granted, Parker looked more like old Dan'l than he did Davy, but he still came across as a somewhat domesticated version of Davy. The show had staying power, however, and twice during its six years on the air it finished in the top 25, in the 1966–67 season and again the following season.

After the series went off the air, Parker retired from show business, invested in real estate, and is now retired from that endeavor after making several million from his investments. In late 1985, he contemplated running for Congress as a Republican, but in March 1986, he announced he would not, apparently preferring to be remembered as Davy Crockett and Daniel Boone rather than take his chances as a politician.

Patricia Blair appeared in the series as Daniel's wife, Rebecca; Darby Hinton was his son, Israel; Dal McKennon was Cincinnatus; Ed Ames appeared as his faithful Indian companion, Mingo; and Veronica Cartwright was his daughter, Jemima. Also featured were Robert Logan as Jericho Jones; Don Pedro Colley as Gideon; ex-football star Roosevelt Grier as Gabe Cooper; country singer Jimmy Dean as Josh Clements, and Albert Salmi as Yadkin.

Operating out of Boonesborough, Kentucky, Boone, along with his traveling buddy Yadkin (1964–65) or Mingo (1964–68), could be counted upon to swiftly dispatch the Indians to the happy hunting grounds when necessary, although he preferred to remain on friendly terms with them. After Dean replaced Ames following the 1968 season, he became Boone's most frequent traveling companion, which seemed to invariably give him an excuse to relax in Cincinnatus' tavern in Boonesborough and discuss his exploits as a fur trapper and daring frontiersman.

Like a few others in the genre, the show was based upon the life of a real character. The real Daniel Boone, however, operated more as a statesman than as a frontiersman, particularly in his later years, although he is credited with opening up Kentucky to settlement.

Using the series as a springboard to a successful recording career, Ed Ames had several Top 40 hits in the 1960s, the biggest of which was "Who Will Answer?" Earlier, he had been a member of the Ames Brothers singing group, which had numerous hit records in the late 1940s and 1950s, the biggest of which were "You, You, You" and "China Doll."

Dean, meanwhile, was a veteran country singer with his own musical variety series on CBS in 1957 and again on ABC from 1963 to 1966. Although his recording career began in the late 1940s, he never had a number one record until the million-selling "Big Bad John" in 1961 began a string of hits which lasted several years.

# Death Valley Days
## *Syndicated*

In case you ever wondered what the Old Ranger's real name was, it was Stanley Adams, and he narrated this long-running series until his death. After Adams died, the host/narrator post was taken over by a then semi-washed-up actor by the name of Ronald Reagan, who would in time go on to bigger and better things. (When Reagan took over, however, the opening narration disappeared, and Reagan was never identified.)

Just as on the earlier radio version of this show, historical events supposedly furnished the source material for the stories, which featured a different guest every week. The series had run on radio beginning in 1930 and lasting until 1945, all the while sponsored by 20 Mule Team Borax and Boraxo, just as it would be on television.

Borrowing from its radio predecessor, the TV show began each week with a team of 20 mules hauling a wagon across the stark desert

**Stanley Adams, or The Old Ranger, as he was known, host of the long-running syndicated series "Death Valley Days." A native of Chicago, Adams hosted the series until his death, at which time the host-narrator role of the series became Ronald Reagan's. At the time of his death, Adams was in his 70s.**

region of Death Valley while the sounds of a bugle faded away, with an anonymous voice intoning, "As the early morning bugle call of covered wagon trains fades away among the echoes, another true Death Valley Days is presented by the famous Borax family of products — 20 Mule Team Borax and Boraxo. Well, Old Ranger, what's your story about?"

# The Deputy
*NBC, September 1959–September 1961*

Very few motion picture stars attempted to make the transition from the wide screen to the small one since they tended to view television with disdain (television did spawn a number of actors who made it big in the movies). However, Henry Fonda tried it, twice; once with "The Smith Family" in 1971–72, and 12 years earlier with this one. Neither proved to be blockbusters.

Judging from the TV Westerns, the Arizona Territory of the 1880s was overrun with United States marshals, but it seemed to be just as overrun with desperadoes. The central theme of the series was the conflict which occurred at times between Chief Marshal Simon Fry (Fonda) and Clay McCord (Allen Case), a young storekeeper who, while a crack shot, was opposed to guns and the subsequent violence that went with them. However, McCord could always be persuaded to act in the capacity of deputy for Herk Lamson (Wallace Ford), the aging marshal of Silver City, when Fry was elsewhere — which was a frequent occurrence.

For the series' second season, Fonda assumed the role of narrator, being featured only when Marshal Fry was in town, which still wasn't all that often. At the same time, the character of Lamson was dropped along with that of McCord's younger sister Fran (Betty Lou Keim). Added to the cast was Sgt. Hap Tasker (Read Morgan), an army sergeant in charge of a supply office in Silver City.

# Destry
*ABC, February 1964–September 1964*

Originally, famed Western novelist Max Brand wrote a book entitled *Destry Rides Again*. In the years that followed, the character was played on film by Tom Mix, James Stewart, and Audie Murphy, and by Andy Griffith on the Broadway stage in a hit musical. The television version featured John Calvin as Harrison Destry and was apparently the straw that broke the camel's back, since the character has yet to resurface.

The TV version presented viewers with the less-than-fearless son of famed lawman Tom Destry, who had been shuttled off to prison on a phony embezzlement charge. Naturally, his son found it necessary to travel around the Old West looking for the perpetrators of the deed which had resulted in dear old Dad's being framed, all the while trying to keep out of trouble himself. Not only could he not keep out of trouble, the series couldn't keep in the ratings. But Calvin surely found some consolation the following year when his next series, the World War II drama "Convoy," lasted all of three months on NBC.

## Dick Powell's Zane Grey Theatre
### CBS, October 1956–September 1962

A Thursday night staple of the CBS lineup from 1958 to 1962, the show aired on Friday night during its first two seasons. Although it was basically an anthology series with Powell acting as host, he more often than not wound up acting in the episodes, particularly during its early years.

As originally conceived and aired, the half-hour series consisted completely of adaptations of the novels and short stories of famed Western writer Zane Grey until the supply eventually ran out. At that time, the series resorted to stories from other writers, although it still carried the "Zane Grey" title.

## Dirty Sally
### CBS, January 1974–July 1974

By the time Jeanette Nolan's portrayal of Sally Fergus appeared, the Western was a dying breed, but that didn't stop her from trying—although someone should have. This series no doubt helped speed up the death of the Western a bit. Sally was a hard-drinking old lady traveling West to the California gold fields in a wagon pulled by a mule named Worthless. She might have made it to California if she hadn't found a way to get either herself or her traveling companion, ex-gunfighter Cyrus Pike (Dack Rambo), involved in everyone's business along the way.

## Dundee and the Culhane
### CBS, September 1967–December 1967

Frontier justice—of a sort—featuring John Mills as the British attorney Dundee, and Sean Garrison as his apprentice, the Culhane. The duo traveled from their law offices in Sausalito, California, to do their part in making the West a better place in which to live.

# Empire
### NBC, September 1962–September 1963

Set in modern-day New Mexico, Jim Redigo (Richard Egan) was the foreman who oversaw the operation of the Garrett empire, which encompassed everything from oil to lumber and, of course, cattle. Spread out over half a million acres, the Garrett holdings proved to be of little interest to viewers.

Also starring in the series were Terry Moore as Constance Garrett, Anne Seymour as Lucia Garrett, a young pre–"Love Story" Ryan O'Neal was Tal Garrett, and Warren Vanders as Chuck. Charles Bronson was Paul Moreno before he became Mr. Macho in the movies.

# Frontier
### NBC, September 1955–September 1956

One of television's earlier and more unsuccessful attempts at an anthology series, this one depicted real people undergoing real trials and tribulations in settling the Old West. Walter Coy was the narrator and also starred in some episodes.

# Frontier Circus
### CBS, October 1961–September 1962

Chill Wills was a veteran actor who had appeared in numerous movies and television series, many of them Westerns. Naturally, there came a time when someone felt he should have a series of his own, and this show was one of the results. (The other result of that thinking was the comedy "The Rounders," which lasted an even shorter period of time.)

Wills was Col. Casey Thompson, and a pre–Bo John Derek was Ben Travis. Together they owned and operated the T and T Circus, which traversed the American West in the late 1800s. Richard Jaeckel, who in recent years has made a career out of seeing how many different shows he can guest star on, was Tony Gentry, the advance man who scouted ahead looking for places where the circus could perform. Storylines revolved around not only the circus characters' relationships with each other but their relationships with the various persons they came into contact with in their travels.

## Frontier Justice
### CBS, *July 1958–September 1958*
### CBS, *July 1959–September 1959*
### CBS, *August 1961–September 1961*

If you saw "Dick Powell's Zane Grey Theatre," you had already seen all the programs aired under this title, since this summer replacement series consisted solely of reruns from Powell's series.

In 1958, it filled in for "December Bride," in 1959 for "The Danny Thomas Show," and in 1961 for the "Zane Grey Theatre." In 1958, it was hosted by Lew Ayres, in 1959 by Melvyn Douglas, and in 1961 by Ralph Bellamy.

## Gabby Hayes
### Syndicated

In addition to being the sidekick and comic relief for a number of movie cowboys, Gabby came into America's living rooms on a weekly basis beginning in 1950, telling tales of the Old West and using clips from old cowboy movies to illustrate his points.

## The Gene Autry Show
### CBS, *July 1950–August 1956*

Roy Rogers may have been the "King of the Cowboys," but Gene Autry was the first of the singing cowboys, not to mention the richest buckaroo to ever jump on a bronc. With his success on the big screen and on record, it was only natural that Autry make the transition to the small screen to solve a few problems associated with the taming of the West and to belt out a few tunes along the way. If the Westerns introduced after 1955 were aimed more or less at the adults, there can be little doubt who this one was for.

Plots — what there were of them, and they were very thin — always could be counted upon to go along the lines of "Gene and his sidekick, Pat Buttram, ride into some town in the West, find a Simon Legree–type character, restore law and order, and ride off to their next adventure." Sometime during the course of each episode, Gene would find an excuse to sing, his horse Champion would perform a couple of tricks to show how well trained he was, and Pat would become embroiled in a ridiculous situation which was always solved by Gene. Sometime during the course of Buttram's problem, he could be counted upon to call out for Autry, and a program wasn't complete without hearing Pat yell out at least once, "Hey, Mr. Artery," in his croaking, froglike voice. Once the problem was solved, there was always a joke, which might go something along the lines of: Autry — How can you be so stupid? Buttram — Well, it ain't easy when you ain't got no brains! Naturally, everyone within earshot enjoyed a good laugh, and hopefully the kids watching at home did as well, no matter how inane the joke was.

A member of the Country Music Hall of Fame in Nashville, Tennessee, Autry made his first record, "No One to Call Me Darling," in 1927. That record, however, was never released, even after Autry became a star in the Texas/Oklahoma area after breaking into the entertainment business with radio station KVOO in Tulsa in 1929. During his recording career — which spanned 41 years, with his last session coming in 1971 — he recorded approximately 400 records for close to a dozen different labels under no fewer than ten different names. His recording of "Here Comes Santa Claus" is the second biggest selling record of all time, surpassed only by Bing Crosby's rendition of "White Christmas."

After making his debut in the movies opposite Ken Maynard in *In Old Santa Fe*, Autry became a kiddie matinee favorite and eventually wound up making 89 feature-length films along with one 15-chapter serial. In 1940, his "Gene Autry's Melody Ranch" began its 16-year run on radio, being interrupted only during World War II when he served in the army air corps as a pilot.

In addition to his films, radio, and television series, Autry found the time to appear at such events as rodeos and became one of the wealthiest of Hollywood actors. In 1961, along with his partner Bob Reynolds, he began operating the California Angels baseball team.

Recorded Theme Music: "Back in the Saddle Again," Gene Autry, Columbia Records.

## The Gray Ghost
*Syndicated*

This Civil War drama glamorized the exploits of Confederate Army commandos under the leadership of Major John Singleton Mosby as portrayed by Tod Andrews. The series tended to be a bit more historically accurate than many, but there was still room for improvement. The real Major Mosby later served in the United States Congress and died around 1920. The TV series died after several years.

## The Guns of Will Sonnett
*ABC, September 1967–September 1969*

Take one old ex–Cavalry scout (grizzled of course, but weren't they all?) named Will Sonnett (Walter Brennan). Add a twentyish grandson named Jeff (Dack Rambo), toss in a notorious gunfighter for a father, James (Jason Evers). Stir, with a helping of elusiveness for the father, and you have the recipe for this series, which saw Will and Jeff traveling throughout the Old West attempting to track down the boy's father. Since Grandpa was Walter Brennan and he was supposedly full of the wisdom to which his 73 years entitled him, you could always count upon him to offer some sage bit of advice at least once per episode.

Brennan, who is probably best remembered for his role of Grandpa McCoy on the long-running situation comedy "The Real McCoys," also found time to begin a recording career in the early 1960s when he recorded the million-selling "Old Rivers" along with a lesser hit, "The Epic Ride of John H. Glenn," which commemorated one of the first space shots. This series represented one of four in which Brennan starred, the others in addition to the aforementioned being "The Tycoon" and "To Rome with Love."

As the father of James Sonnett, he never saw his son in the series (although James did appear briefly in a few episodes). Mostly Will and Jeff were always showing up someplace where he had been recently, since there were a large number of people who had come in contact with him. For a touch of finality to the series, in the last episode Will and Jeff came across the man who claimed to have killed James, but you never really found out if he was telling the truth or not.

# Gunslinger
### CBS, February 1961–September 1961

Following the Civil War, everybody moved West, or so it seemed. Why else would the area need such a large number of peace officers? Add to that list, Cord (Tony Young), a fast gun (of course) who worked undercover for Capt. Zachary Wingate (Preston Foster), the commandant of Fort Scott, New Mexico. Pico McGuire (Charles Gray) and Billy Urchin (Dee Pollock) were Cord's compadres and often accompanied him on his peacekeeping treks throughout the area.

# Gunsmoke
### CBS, September 1955–September 1975

It turned out to be the grandaddy of them all by the time Matt Dillon laid down his trusty six-gun on September 1, 1975. Beginning on September 10 some 20 years earlier, Matt, Kitty, Doc, Chester, Festus and the assorted residents of Dodge City, Kansas, came to epitomize the Western and subsequently gave it a new meaning: Adults could watch and enjoy as well as their offspring. One of two so-called "adult Westerns" to take to the air in 1955, it was actually preceded by "The Life and Legend of Wyatt Earp" by four days, but in the end, the adventures of the Dodge City crew managed to outlast the adventures of the real-life cowboy by 14 years.

Of the nine "regular" cast members, in addition to the 6-foot, 7-inch James Arness, who played Matt, only Milburn Stone, playing Doc Adams, was with the show from start to finish. Amanda Blake as Miss Kitty Russell departed after 19 seasons, and with no female lead character, the series expired after one season. Other cast members came and went throughout the years. Glenn Strange, as Sam, the bartender, poured drinks at Kitty's Long Branch Saloon from 1962 to 1974. Former big-band singer Ken Curtis was the lovable, scruffy Festus Haggen who wandered the streets of Dodge from 1964 to 1975. Matt's original sidekick left over from the days of radio, Chester Goode (although he was called Chester Proudfoot on radio), was played by Dennis Weaver from 1955 to 1964, but it seemed as though he was around for much longer. Other regulars of duration included Buck Taylor as Newly O'Brien from 1969 to 1975; a very young Burt Reynolds as Quint Asper from 1962 to 1965; and Roger Ewing as Thad Greenwood in 1966 to 1967.

Stepping into the role originated by William Conrad on CBS Radio in 1952, Arness was the second choice of actors to appear as Matt Dillon, the role originally having been offered to Hollywood legend John Wayne. While Wayne did introduce the first episode, that was the extent of his involvement with the series. Arness, a Minneapolis native, had been wounded at Anzio during World War II and moved to Hollywood following the war; several small movie parts there led to his being offered the role of the space creature in the movie "The Thing," and the rest, as they say, is history.

Weaver, who had narrowly missed making the United States Olympic Track and Field team in 1948, was, like Arness, a television newcomer. After leaving the series, he starred in the kiddie-oriented program "Gentle Ben," the detective series "Stone," another kid's series, "Kentucky Jones," and the hit detective series "McCloud," in which he portrayed a Taos, New Mexico, marshal on loan to the New York Police Department from whom he was supposed to learn modern crime-fighting methods. Combined, none of the series lasted as long as the series which gave him his start. In recent years, he has become a semi-regular on the cornpone version of "Laugh-In," "Hee Haw," and has recorded several country music record albums.

For Blake and Stone, "Gunsmoke" marked the extent of their involvement with series television, while Curtis popped up on the prime-time Western soap opera "The Yellow Rose" in the early 1980s, playing a role somewhat similar to that of Festus. Reynolds, of course, went on to become a Hollywood good-old-boy legend and box office smash after appearing in two less-than-memorable detective series, "Dan August" and "Hawk."

"Gunsmoke" ran in a half-hour format during its first four years, 1955–59, first going up against "The George Gobel Show." It was expanded to an hour in 1960, while reruns of the original half-hour version were aired earlier in the week under the title "Marshal Dillon" for three years.

By its second year, the program had moved into the top ten for the season, settling in at number eight. From 1957 to 1961, it was the top-rated program, and with the exception of the period from 1964 to 1967 and its final season, the series remained in the top 20 throughout its run. "Gunsmoke" was one of only three Westerns (along with "Bonanza" and "Wagon Train") to be rated number one for an entire season.

Set in Dodge City in the 1880s, early plots revolved around Matt, Doc, Kitty, and Chester. No one ever really knew what the true relationship was between Matt and Kitty, although it had been spelled out much more explicitly on radio. In short, on radio she was someone whom Matt found it necessary to visit once in a while—a prostitute. On TV, though, that angle was toned down considerably, and Matt and Kitty never so much as went on a date, let alone slept together.

Unlike its radio counterpart, which ran until 1961, the television version of "Gunsmoke" tended to be somewhat mild. On radio, Conrad portrayed Dillon as a somewhat sad, lonely, and tragic figure who was tough as nails and who would periodically wind up on the losing end of a fight. The TV version was much more sympathetic.

The simple format with which the series started gave way to the tackling of social issues in the 1960s in an attempt to gain "relevance." Matt was sometimes seen on the screen for less than a minute at the beginning of an episode and again at the end, a situation which may have contributed in part to the show's decline in the ratings in the mid-60s. Throughout the duration of its 20-year run, though, the one constant was Matt Dillon, who, like Superman, stood for truth, justice, and the American way.

Recorded Theme Music: Although no vocal version of the main theme was ever heard, there was a vocal version recorded by the Prairie Chiefs on RCA Children's Bluebird Records. Despite the series' longevity, this was the only version of the theme ever recorded.

# Have Gun, Will Travel
*CBS, September 1957–September 1963*

His calling card bore the figure of a knight from a chess set and was inscribed simply, "Have Gun, Will Travel . . . Wire Paladin, San Francisco." From the beginning you knew this was one hombre you didn't want to tangle with, particularly if you were an outlaw. Every Saturday night for six years, Paladin (he had no first name) would embark upon a new adventure. Audiences loved it, catapulting the show into the fourth-most-watched program that first season and into the number three spot for the next two years.

Although it was not generally known, if you wanted one of Paladin's cards, you could write to the studio and request one. While they weren't autographed, at the time it was an ego trip to be carrying around a "Have Gun, Will Travel" card . . . just like Paladin.

With the late Richard Boone in the title role, the series was perhaps one of the two or three most outstanding of its genre. It usually featured above-average writing, and Boone was one of the better, and most underrated, actors of the period on television. A seventh-generation nephew of frontiersman Daniel Boone, he had been an aerial gunner in the navy during World War II and was aboard the aircraft carrier *Intrepid* when it was torpedoed. Prior to becoming Paladin — the role for which he is best remembered — the 6-foot, 2-inch Boone had twice been nominated for an Emmy while starring on "Medic," an early medical drama.

Moving from the hospital to the Old West, as Paladin he had one simple motto by which he lived: "I never draw my gun, unless I intend to use it." When he did use it, the bad guys never stood a chance. Calling San Francisco's Hotel Carlton home, the fashionably dressed Paladin was a West Point graduate who was once an army officer in charge of weapons. After leaving the army, he had dedicated himself to enjoying the good life while hiring himself out as a soldier of fortune to insure that the good life continued uninterrupted. Paladin, dressed entirely in black, also possessed a sense of ethics which at times dictated he turn those who hired him over to the law, if it turned out they were the true guilty parties.

Each show usually began with the cultured Paladin receiving a message from a prospective client, brought to him by the hotel's Oriental houseboy, Hey Boy (Kam Tong). During the 1960–61 season, Tong was busy with the less-than-successful series "The Garlund Touch," and during his absence, the weekly message was delivered by Hey Girl (Lisa Lu).

Recorded Theme Music: "The Ballad of Paladin," Johnny Western, Columbia Records (vocal version). "The Ballad of Paladin," Duane Eddy, RCA Victor Records (instrumental).

# Hec Ramsey
*NBC, October 1972–August 1974*

One of the four rotating series in NBC's "Sunday Mystery Movie," "Hec Ramsey" was the only Western involved in the quartet, which also featured Dennis Weaver in "McCloud," Peter Falk in "Columbo," and Rock Hudson and Susan St. James in "McMillan and Wife."

Ramsey (Richard Boone), a former gunfighter, arrived in New Prospect, Oklahoma, around the turn of the century to serve as a deputy to Sheriff Oliver B. Stamp (Richard Lenz), who was more than just a little bit apprehensive about his new partner's reputation. Added to that was the fact that Ramsey had become somewhat enamored of the then infant science of criminology and spent years learning all he could about it and the new techniques available for apprehending criminals. Although he still carried a gun and could use it if necessary, he preferred instead to utilize the new technology, which included such items as fingerprinting equipment, scales, and magnifying glasses, an approach Stamp at first found novel, but one he eventually learned to live with.

Also starring in the series were veteran character actor Harry Morgan as Doctor Amos Coogan and Dennis Rucker as Arne Tornquist.

# The High Chaparral
*NBC, September 1967–September 1971*

Imagine moving the Ponderosa or the Barkley Ranch to Arizona. Marry Ben to the daughter of a wealthy Mexican cattle baron, and give him a brother and a brother-in-law instead of three sons. What you get is "The High Chaparral": another sprawling adventure on a ranch, with brothers, ranch hands, in-laws, and the usual assortment of characters, both good and bad, you could expect to find in the Arizona Territory. But, while there were many similarities in "Bonanza," "The Big Valley," and this series, there were a number of notable differences also.

Led by Big John Cannon (the late Leif Erickson) and his brother Buck (Cameron Mitchell), the Cannon clan, along with Big John's in-laws, the Montoyas, fought off the trials and tribulations one might expect to find during the 1870s while fervently attempting to establish a cattle empire in that part of the Southwest. Herein lies one major difference between this show and its counterparts: the Cartwrights and Barkleys had their fortunes made, and you knew they would never be hurting for money. The Cannons, on the other hand, while never starving, did have more than their fair share of monetary problems, and a number of scripts during the series' run dealt with this actuality.

In addition to Erickson and Mitchell, other series mainstays were Manolito Montoya (Henry Darrow), Victoria Cannon (Linda Cristal), Sam Butler, the foreman (Don Collier) and Joe, a ranch hand (Robert Hoy). Billy Blue Cannon (Mark Slade), John's son by his first wife, helped form a part of the Cannon household for the first three years before being dropped prior to the start of what was to be the final season. Don Sebastian Montoya (Frank Silvera), Victoria's father, was also written out as having died when Silvera did, in fact, die. Also eliminated prior to the last season were the roles of the ranch hands, Pedro (Roberto Contreras) and another one-name character, Reno (Ted Markland), as the series proceeded with a major overhaul. Joining the cast for what turned out to be its final season was a halfbreed, Wind (Rudy Ramos).

Considering the fact that it was something of a clone of the other family-on-a-ranch series, this show remained a cut above average, thanks in part to the frequency of stories featuring Buck and Manolito, a duo who would have been much happier playing cards and drinking than working on the ranch or punching cattle. However, when the occasion called for them to earn their keep by performing ranch-type duties, they were affable participants, despite their protests that they had other, more important things to do, chief among them, chasing women.

# Hondo
*ABC, September 1961–December 1961*

In the beginning there was Louis L'Amour's novel, *Hondo*. It gave rise to the classic John Wayne Western movie of the same name in 1953. Fourteen years later, Ralph Taeger portrayed a TV version of cavalry scout Hondo Lane, and the role hasn't been reprised since. If all that sounds familiar, Hondo was following in Destry's footsteps.

Hondo, a loner, along with his dog, Sam, attempted to prevent bloodshed between the Indians and the settlers, not to mention assorted gunmen and bandits around Fort Lowell. A former captain in the Confederate Cavalry, Hondo had lived with the Apaches and married the chief's daughter only to see her killed by the army in a massacre. Why he later sided with the army was never explained, but you can only do so much in four months. Capt. Richards (Gary Clarke) was the commandant at Fort Lowell; Buffalo Baker (Noah Beery, Jr.) was the scout; Angie Dow (Kathie Browne) was Richards' romantic interest; and Johnny (Buddy Foster) was Angie's nine-year-old son.

If ever a person was snake-bitten, it had to be Taeger. His other attempts at weekly series television left much to be desired; he starred in "Klondike" and "Acapulco," but both bit the dust after a short period of time.

# Hopalong Cassidy
*NBC, June 1949–December 1951*

Hoppy (William Boyd) was one of the original Western heroes. Even after his series ended its network run, he was seen in syndication for a number of years, never aging, always the silver-haired king of the range showing up on his horse, Topper, in just the nick of time to right all the wrongs.

No dummy, Boyd hocked all his belongings in the late 1940s when television was still in its infancy and bought—for $300,000—all the rights to the more than 60 Hopalong Cassidy "B" movies he had starred in. For a short period of time, he found himself virtually dead broke, but it was a situation which was to change drastically.

As originally conceived, Hoppy was an uncouth, hard-drinking relic of the Old West, but Boyd made the hero into a knight of the range, a straight-shootin' moralist who never kissed the ladies, but who would definitely help them across the street. And, unlike many other Western heroes, he never took a drink, believed in fair play, and presented the epitome of all that was good and righteous.

This image was in direct contrast to Boyd's own life. Born in Ohio in 1898, he became a star through his success in such Cecil B. DeMille epics as *King of Kings*, *Two Arabian Nights* and *The Volga Boatman*. His success led him to enjoy a hedonistic lifestyle, indulging in wine, women, and song to excess, drinking, gambling, purchasing expensive playthings and estates, and living the good life, only to see it crumble into ashes with the Depression of 1929 and the advent of talking pictures. Although his voice was naturally suited to the talkies, his career was ruined when another actor named William Boyd was arrested for the possession of gambling equipment and illegal whiskey. Even as the other Boyd was being arraigned, newspapers ran photos of the wrong Boyd. The publicity resulted in cancelled movie contracts and a career on the skids even after the mistake was cleared up.

Four years later, Boyd saw his star once again rise when he made the first of the Hopalong Cassidy movies, changed his personal habits, married for the fifth and final time in 1937, and gave up his drinking and carousing, adapting the Hoppy image to his own life.

Originally, the adventures of Hoppy shown on the small screen were edited-down versions of the movies, with narration and a new scene or two added for the sake of variety, in case you had seen it on the big screen and recognized it. Eventually though, the old movies ran out, and Boyd found it necessary to take to the range once again, adding a sidekick, Red Connors (Edgar Buchanan). From there, it was all pretty much your standard Western fare, with Hoppy — who was supposedly the foreman of the Bar-20 Ranch, chasing the villains across the range week after week. But the kids ate it up, and Hoppy was definitely for the kids and no one else.

Shortly before his death on September 12, 1972, Boyd sold out his stock of films and the rights for a reported $70,000,000 — all of which came as the result of television and a shrewd marketing campaign he developed for Hopalong Cassidy merchandise for the kids. For example, he was one of the first movie and TV characters to appear on what had previously been reserved for baseball players — the bubblegum trading card. Today, a set of 238 Hopalong Cassidy cards issued in 1950 when the Hoppy craze was at its peak is worth about $350 in mint condition. The two different wrappers alone are worth about $30 each. For a while, the Hopalong Cassidy craze was the in thing, as wild and

Earl Holliman is no doubt remembered more for costarring with Angie Dickinson in "Police Story" from 1974 to 1978, but in 1959–60 he was Sundance in the short-lived "Hotel de Paree." Note the silver discs on the hatband, which were used to blind his foes in a gunfight.

frantic as the Davy Crockett craze was to become a few years down the road.

## Hotel de Paree
### *CBS, October 1959–September 1960*

Earl Holliman — who is probably remembered more for costarring with Angie Dickinson in "Police Story" from 1974 to 1978 — was Sundance, the fast gun in residence at the Hotel de Paree in Georgetown,

Colorado, around 1870. Sundance returned to the hotel after spending 17 years in prison for killing a man, only to find upon arriving that it was now being run by his relatives Annette Deveraux (Jeanette Nolan) and her niece Monique (Judi Meredith). If you remember the highly polished silver discs Sundance wore around his hatband to blind his foes, you remember the high point of the series.

## How the West Was Won
### ABC, February 1978–August 1978

Another John Wayne movie that found its way to the small screen (like *Hondo* and *The Cowboys*), this one failed to ride the range for an extended period of time despite the high quality of the scripts, better-than-average acting, and consistently high ratings. It also offered James Arness as Zeb Macahan, proving that there was life after "Gunsmoke," however brief. It was also the last Western to appear on television until the abortive attempts in the 1980s with "Bret Maverick" and "Wildside" and signaled an end to the Golden Age of TV Westerns. In addition, it was the last of its genre to be listed among the ratings leaders for a season.

Zeb was a former mountain man who had spent ten years in the rugged Dakota Territory prior to returning to Virginia, where his brother's family was getting ready to make the move West. Shortly after hitting the trail, the Civil War broke out, his brother Timothy returned East, Timothy's wife Kate was killed in an accident, and Uncle Zeb was suddenly in the position of being guardian to the kids.

Adding to the somewhat soap-operaish plot already in existence were the kids themselves: Luke (Bruce Boxleitner) was a fugitive from the law after killing three men in self-defense. His sister, Laura (Kathryn Holcomb), was seen as fair game for every eligible bachelor the clan came across; another sister, Jessie (Vicki Schreck), was the 12-year-old you could expect to find in a family the size of the Macahans; and Josh (William Kirby Cullen) was a teenager who was anxious to prove he was a man. In addition, Aunt Molly Culhane (Fionnula Flanagan), Kate's widowed sister (convenient, huh?), came from Boston to help out.

# The Iron Horse
*ABC, September 1966–January 1968*

After he made sure that Wells Fargo was in good hands after starring in "Tales of Wells Fargo" for five years, Dale Robertson moved from stagecoaches to railroads. The one he was associated with in this series, however, wasn't just any railroad. It was the Buffalo Pass, Scalplock and Defiance Line; it was on the verge of bankruptcy and was owned by Robertson who, as Ben Calhoun, had won the railroad in a poker game. However, his winnings proved not to be such a good deal, for not only was the railroad almost bankrupt, it was only half built, and it was up to him to finish the job.

Along with his construction engineer Dave Tarrant (Gary Collins), crewman Nils (Roger Torrey), and a young orphan, Barnabas Rogers (Bob Random), who served as his clerk, Calhoun fought off the expected Indians and desperadoes who attempted to insure the failure of the railroad. During the second and final season, Julie Parsons (Ellen McRae) was added to the cast as the freight station operator and proprietor of the Scalplock General Store.

After starring in three short-lived series, "Born Free," "The Sixth Sense," and "The Wackiest Ship in the Army," Collins — who is married to former Miss America Mary Ann Mobley — moved on to the talk show circuit as host for the syndicated "Hour Magazine."

# Jefferson Drum
*NBC, April 1958–April 1959*

Drum (Jeff Richards) was the editor of the local newspaper in the mining town of Jubilee, which was somewhere out West during the 1850s. Although the peace-loving Drum preferred to set a good example for his son Joey (Eugene Martin), he would strap on his guns and face his adversaries if necessary.

He was aided in his attempts to help out the law-abiding citizenry by his printer, Lucius Cain (Cyril Delavanti), and by Big Ed (Robert Stevenson), the bartender at the local saloon.

Jeff Richards' sole experience at series television came in the late 1950s when he portrayed the editor of a local newspaper, Jefferson Drum, in the short-lived series of the same name.

# Johnny Ringo
### CBS, October 1959–September 1960

Any similarities between the exploits of the real-life Johnny Ringo and those of the one on this series were no doubt purely coincidental, but just like in the real world, Johnny Ringo was portrayed as a gunfighter who saw the error of his ways and became a lawman.

Don Durant was Ringo, while Mark Goddard was his deputy Cully. Between the two of them, they attempted to bring law and order to Velardi, Arizona. Laura Thomas (Karen Sharpe) was Ringo's love interest, and her father, Case (Terence de Marney), ran the general store when he wasn't off on a bender someplace.

While the series marked the end of the trail for Durant, his costars managed to hang around for a few more years. Goddard was featured in the short-lived "Many Happy Returns" in 1964–65 and went on to play Don West in the science-fiction series "Lost in Space." Sharpe was to be featured periodically in "I Dream of Jeannie" in 1965–66.

## Judge Roy Bean
### Syndicated

Before he moved on to become the lovable Uncle Joe on "Petticoat Junction," the late Edgar Buchanan received his chance to move from the role of sidekick to starring role when he portrayed the legendary Judge Roy Bean, "the law West of the Pecos."

The real Judge Bean was nowhere near as kindly and sweet as he was made out to be on this series. In fact, the real Bean would just as soon hang a man who looked at him crosseyed, but it's unlikely any hangings ever took place on the series.

Also appearing in the series were Jack Beutel, Jackie Loughery, and Russell Hayden, formerly the star of "The Marshal of Gunsight Pass."

## Klondike
### NBC, October 1960–February 1961

There was something about Ralph Taeger; either the viewing public didn't like him, or he was just unfortunate to star in several series which featured awful scriptwriting and weren't believable.

"Klondike" placed Taeger in Skagway, Alaska, during the Gold Rush of 1897–99. As Mike Halliday, he spent a great deal of time attempting to outwit the obligatory villain, Jeff Durain (James Coburn), a gambler and dastardly no-account type whose attempts to make the easy buck usually put him on the wrong side of the law. Durain also ran a hotel, where the miners could lose their earnings gambling in the casino in games which were somewhat less than honest.

But wait, there's more. In a classic confrontation, viewers were presented with a Bad Hotel vs. Good Hotel plot, with the latter being run by Kathy O'Hara (Mari Blanchard). And, of course, there was also the usual lady friend — in this case, Durain's girlfriend and accomplice, Goldie (Joi Lansing).

Taeger's bad luck with series television continued in the sunny climes of "Acapulco" and again in "Hondo"; both series bombed. Coburn, of course, went on to star in such movies as *In Like Flint* and *Our Man Flint* and is currently the televised spokesman for Master Card. Believe it or not, he co-starred in the ill-fated "Acapulco." After that, he gave up series television, but who could blame him?

# Kung Fu
## *ABC, October 1972–June 1975*

In the late 1960s and early 1970s, kung fu was the "in" thing; many people who would never have dreamed of taking up any form of physical exercise suddenly become devotees of this ancient form of Chinese martial arts. Many of them had also seen a great many of the Bruce Lee movies, which featured almost nonstop kung fu action. The times were ripe for those seeking escapism from the pressures of the real world. In the Oriental mysticism surrounding kung fu, many people found their answer to whatever was troubling them. Or at least they thought they did.

Network executives, ever quick to latch onto a craze (there was even a hit record, Carl Douglas' "Kung Fu Fighting"), decided there must be something to all this kicking and yelling. They combined the best of two worlds and gave the world a kung fu Western. What's even more amazing is that the series managed to last three years.

Making its debut as an "ABC Movie of the Week," like most pilots, the movie attracted a great deal of attention, and the series was born. The non–Oriental David Carradine — son of noted horror movie actor John Carradine — appeared in the role of Caine (full name: Kwai Chang Caine), a loner who had been forced to kill a member of the Chinese royal family and who, when not searching for the secrets of the universe, spent his time searching for a long-lost brother in the American West.

A shaven-headed Buddhist monk, Caine was born of mixed parentage and was subsequently raised as an orphan at the Shaolin Temple. There he was tutored in a philosophy which stressed inner harmony and the practice of a life of nonviolence. Naturally, he was also taught kung fu, since one never knew when it might come in handy.

Fleeing to the American West, Caine was often an outcast since he was Chinese—or at least appeared Chinese—but undeterred, he would bow his head and give the audience that week's particular piece of Oriental philosophy. Since he was well-versed in the martial arts, the use of a gun was naturally taboo. When he was placed in a compromising situation which was at least once per week, he took on the bad guys martial arts style, usually in slow motion.

Frequently—at least once per show, or so it seemed—there would be a flashback episode with the young Caine (Radames Pera), receiving a liberal dosage of Oriental philosophy from his teachers, Master Po (Keye Luke) and Master Kan (Philip Ahn). Usually, this would be just prior to the Big Fight of the Week.

In the series' final season, Caine was occasionally seen with a female American cousin, Margit (Season Hubley), whose appearance was obviously calculated to boost the sagging ratings. It didn't help.

Although Caine supposedly was out there searching for his brother, he apparently took time out for other activities as well: A 1986 TV movie which reprised the series gave him a son.

Interestingly enough, David Carradine dropped out of the Hollywood lifestyle and more or less adopted the same mystical attitude as Caine.

# Lancer
## CBS, September 1968–June 1970

Whether by design or accident, there seemed to be an inordinately large number of ranchers in California who had a great deal of difficulty holding onto their land; this series portrayed one such rancher. It was primarily the story of Murdoch Lancer (Andrew Duggan), who was unable to defend his cattle and sheep ranch against the unscrupulous local undesirables despite the help of a young ward, Teresa O'Brien (Elizabeth Baur). As a result, word went out to his two sons, Scott (Wayne Maunder) and Johnny (James Stacy), for help. Although the two had never met, being the result of two different marriages, the conflict between them and their methods of resolving problems provided material for a number of stories.

Johnny was a gunfighter and drifter who had spent the better part of his life in and out of trouble in the border towns. Scott was a sophisticated college graduate who was living the life of a gentleman in Boston.

Veteran character actor Paul Brinegar was added to the cast in the role of Jelly Hoskins, a grizzled old ranch hand (like most old scouts, weren't most old ranch hands grizzled?), for the second season.

Duggan who also starred or co-starred in such series as "Bourbon Street Beat," "Room for One More," and "Twelve O'Clock High," can now be seen almost daily pitching life insurance for senior citizens.

# Laramie
### NBC, September 1959–September 1963

For four years, the Sherman brothers, Slim (John Smith) and Andy (Bobby Crawford, Jr.), attempted to maintain the family ranch following the death of their father in the late 1800s in, you guessed it, Wyoming. But when a character appeared who had stronger viewer appeal than Andy, the latter's days were numbered, although he did manage to stay around for two of the four years the show was on the air. In the very first episode, Jess Harper (Robert Fuller), a drifter, appeared, and the audience reaction to him was so much stronger than to Andy that poor Andy's appearances became less and less frequent until he was written out of the show entirely in 1961.

Other characters appearing in the series, which was a Tuesday night staple during its run, included Jonesy (Hoagy Carmichael, 1959–60), Mort Corey (Stuart Randall, 1960–63), Mike Williams (Dennis Holmes, 1961–63), and Daisy Cooper (Spring Byington, 1961–63).

Besides raising cattle (didn't everyone?), the ranch, which had provided only a meager living prior to the death of Sherman's father, also served as a relay station for the stage lines that ran in and out of Laramie, which was close by. This naturally accounted for many of the characters who appeared on the show and caused problems for Sherman and Harper.

The series appearance was Hoagy Carmichael's sole shot at series television, but he had already made his fortune and is best remembered for writing the classic songs "Stardust" and "Georgia on My Mind," the latter of which was to become the state song of Georgia.

# Laredo
*NBC, September 1965–September 1967*

This was one of a series of programs that featured the legendary Texas Rangers. It also was played with a sense of humor, but not with the sense of stupidity displayed by "F Troop" (although the potential was surely there; the producers and writers should be credited with having the good sense not to let it happen).

Most of the humor in the series derived from jokes made at the expense of former Union Army officer Reese Bennett (Neville Brand), who was in his forties when he joined the Rangers and Company B in the post–Civil War era. His much younger partners were Joe Riley (William Smith), a former gunfighter (weren't most of the good guys?) who was attempting to steer clear of the authorities in the other territories, and Chad Cooper (Peter Brown), who had joined the Rangers in an attempt to continue his search for the gunrunners who sold arms to the Mexicans who had killed most of his friends and comrades on the Border Patrol. Overseeing their activities and assignments was Captain Parmalee (Philip Carey), the only person in the series who was normal. Erik Hunter (Robert Wolders) joined the crew as another Ranger in its second and final season.

# Law of the Plainsman
*NBC, October 1959–September 1960*

Since he looked somewhat like the American public's concept of an Indian and had played one on "Broken Arrow," what better way to typecast the Lebanese Michael Ansara than to have him continue in the same kind of role? As a result, Ansara wound up portraying Deputy United States Marshal Sam Buckhart, an Apache who was attempting to bring law and order to the New Mexico Territory in the 1880s.

It seems that Sam (at that time known as Buck Heart) had nursed back to health a cavalry captain who had been wounded in an ambush. Several years later, the captain died, and Sam found himself the beneficiary in the captain's will. The catch? The money was to be used for an education at private schools and Harvard University, hardly places where you would expect to find an Indian during that period.

Obviously, he persevered, and following his graduation, he returned to the New Mexico Territory determined to become a United States Marshal. Serving under Marshal Andy Morrison (Dayton

*Left:* Another Warner Brothers Western, "Lawman" featured Peter Brown as Johnny McKay from 1958 to 1962. John Russell was Brown's mentor in the series. *Right:* Hugh O'Brian achieved his greatest and longest-lasting fame as legendary United States Marshal Wyatt Earp. While "The Life and Legend of Wyatt Earp" enjoyed a six-year run on television, O'Brian's only other attempt at series television, "Search" in 1972–73, had nowhere near the staying power.

Lummis) in Santa Fe, Sam attempted to reconcile the Indians and the white man while at the same time fighting the ever-present desperadoes.

Tess Logan (Gina Gillespie) was an eight-year-old orphan he had rescued following a stagecoach accident, and both she and Sam roomed at Martha Commager's (Nora Marlowe) rooming house.

# Lawman
### *ABC, October 1958–October 1962*

From the same studios, Warner Brothers, that gave television viewers "Sugarfoot," "Cheyenne," "77 Sunset Strip," and a host of others, came "Lawman" with John Russell as Marshal Dan Troop. And, for a change, there were no contract hassles with the studio; no walkouts, no threatening to quit. The star stayed with his series, and Russell and Warners lived in harmony throughout the duration of the series' four-year run.

Aided by his deputy, Johnny McKay (Peter Brown), the mustachioed Troop brought the desperadoes to justice in a series that was devoid of gimmicks or tricks and just offered week after week of Western adventure.

Also appearing in the series were Peggy Castle as Lily Merrill and Dan Sheridan as Jake.

# The Legend of Jesse James
### *ABC, September 1965–September 1966*

Were the James boys—good old Frank and Jesse—really the bad guys truth and legend knew them to be, or were they a pair of misunderstood Old West Robin Hoods, victims of a society which drove them to rob trains and banks, not to mention killing a few people along the way? If you can believe the latter, you would, no doubt, sit in front of the television set on Monday evenings and feel a surge of pity for the poor misguided boys. On the other hand, if you knew the slightest bit of Western history, you would dismiss this show for what it was: mindless drivel.

ABC's attempt to make heroes out of this less-than-charming duo (not to mention the fun-loving Younger Brothers, Cole and Bob) died after one full season, but should have died much earlier. Even "Three's Company" looks intelligent when compared to this one.

Christopher Jones had the less-than-enviable task of making Jesse appear romantic and handsome, while Allen Case (who was opposed to violence when he appeared in the series "The Deputy") portrayed the older and wiser Frank. John Milford and Tim McIntire were Cole and Bob Younger, with Robert Wilke appearing as Marshal Sam Corbett.

With the exception of McIntire, who popped up on "Rich Man, Poor Man" in the 1976–77 miniseries, the other members of the cast all rode off into the sunset after this series and haven't been heard from since.

# The Life and Legend of Wyatt Earp
*ABC, September 1955–September 1961*

Judging from the number of continuing characters introduced in the series during the course of its six-year run, you would have thought it was a prime-time soap opera. No fewer than 23 different characters appeared at one time or another on a regular basis. Fortunately for the viewers, most of the characters only stayed around for a year or two.

This show was the first of the so-called "adult Westerns," preceding the premiere of "Gunsmoke" by four days. Three times during its run, the program placed in the top 25 for the season, going as high as number six in 1957–58.

Of all the characters, only Hugh O'Brian as Earp was a constant. Doc Holliday (1957–61), played by Douglas Fowley and for a short period of time in 1959 by Myron Healy, was the only other character of any real duration. Other continuing characters included: Bat Masterson (Mason Alan Dinehart III, 1955–57); Ben Thompson (Denver Pyle, 1955–56); Bill Thompson (Hal Baylor, 1955–56); Abbie Crandall (Gloria Talbot, 1955–56); Marsh Murdock (Don Haggerty, 1955–56); Doc Fabrique (Douglas Fowley, 1955–56); Jim "Dog" Kelly (Paul Brinegar and Ralph Sanford, 1956–59); Mayor Hoover (Selmer Jackson, 1956–57); Deputy Hal Norton (William Tanner, 1957–58); Kate Holliday (Carol Stone, 1957–58); Shotgun Gibbs (Morgan Woodward, 1958–61); Morgan Earp (Dirk London, 1959–61); Virgil Earp (John Anderson, 1959–61); Nellie Cashman (Randy Stuart, 1959–60); Ike "Old Man" Clanton (Trevor Bardette, 1959–61); Emma Clanton (Carol Thurston, 1959–60); Sheriff Johnny Behan (1959, Lash LaRue; 1959–61, Steve Brodie); Curley Bill Brocius (William Phipps, 1959–61); Johnny Ringo (Britt Lomond, 1960–61); Mayor Clum (Stacy Harris, 1960–61); and Doc Goodfellow (Damian O'Flynn, 1959–61). If nothing else, the program should be given a great deal of credit for keeping a number of actors employed.

There was in fact a real Wyatt Earp. He bore absolutely no physical resemblance to O'Brian, but in the world of the TV Western, nobody really cared. And the real Earp did cross paths with a number of the Old West's more notorious characters such as Holliday and Brocius. The real Earp was the marshal at Ellsworth and Dodge City, Kansas, and Tombstone, Arizona. He, along with his brothers, Virgil and Morgan, and their good friend Doc Holliday, did have a shootout with the Clanton gang at the O.K. Corral, although any resemblance between the numerous Hollywood glamorized versions and the actual event is purely a matter of coincidence. So the program could be said to be somewhat historically accurate, with the usual liberties being taken for the sake of hoped-for high ratings.

It made no difference, for example, that few of the televised gunfights took more than one bullet — two at the most — to finish. In truth, however, most of the gunfights that took place in the Old West wounded more bystanders than participants, since the guns were more often than not highly inaccurate, and the odds were against hitting the person you were shooting at with just one shot. Obviously, no one would sit still through a gunfight that lasted 15 minutes or more, so from the earliest days, Hollywood felt it necessary to take liberties with historical actuality.

Beginning with the initial episode in which Earp became the marshal of Ellsworth, the story line developed with him moving on to Dodge City for the second year and eventually on to Tombstone in time for the series' fifth season. In Tombstone, Earp came up against the Clanton gang, which more or less ruled the Arizona Territory, right down to having their own hand-picked sheriff, Johnny Behan. Earp, as marshal, could not allow the situation to stand pat. Story lines in the last two seasons revolved around his numerous efforts to remove the Clantons and lessen their stranglehold on the territory. As might be expected, sooner or later, the O.K. Corral battle had to be fought. In a five-part story that wrapped up the series, Earp, along with his brothers and old buddy Doc Holliday, put the Clanton gang out of business permanently. In the process, they played out a satisfactory ending for the series in which all the loose ends were wrapped up in one neat and tidy package.

Earp's trademark pistol was a "Buntline Special," a .45 with an extra long barrel, presented to him by the writer and showman Ned Buntline (Lloyd Corrigan), who would pop up occasionally to check on things and gather material for another dime novel on the Old West. Earp would have preferred to maintain law and order without firearms, but if the situation called for him to use a gun, it was comforting to know one was available.

Recorded Theme Music: "Wyatt Earp," Shorty Long, RCA Children's Bluebird Records. This was not the same version played over the credits on the show, that unreleased version being performed by the Ken Darby Singers.

Other Music of Interest: "Hugh O'Brian Sings," ABC Paramount

Records. A four-song extended play record of Western songs performed by O'Brian. The songs had absolutely nothing to do with the series, but the record is worth mentioning because it is apparently quite rare.

# The Life and Times of Grizzly Adams
## NBC, February 1977–July 1978

Not exactly your standard Western by any stretch of the imagination since there were no gunfights, Indian wars, cattle stampedes, or bank robberies, this show still featured Indians, mountain men, and a bear named Ben, all of whom coexisted in the Western United States in the mid-1800s.

Based somewhat loosely upon the exploits of the real Grizzly Adams (who died in 1860), the TV version had him wrongly accused of a crime, at which time he retreated to the wilderness, built a cabin, and attempted to live in harmony with Mother Nature. The real Grizzly Adams, meanwhile, had gone bankrupt following a series of less-than-successful business transactions, abandoned his wife and children, and spent his years in the Sierra Nevada, hunting and killing animals as well as capturing some for zoos. (Incidentally, there was a real Ben as well; he died in a San Francisco zoo Adams had opened in the 1850s.) Like his TV counterpart, despite the hunting and killing, the real Grizzly did love animals and cared for them.

Dan Haggerty, who portrayed Adams, was a former animal trainer. He played the same role in the feature film which gave the TV series its title, and a similar role in *The Adventures of Frontier Fremont*. Denver Pyle, who appeared as his friend Mad Jack, was also in both theatrical releases. Also appearing were Don Shanks as Adams' Indian blood brother, Nakuma, and John Bishop as Robbie Cartman, the son of a farmer who lived in the area.

# The Lone Ranger
## ABC, September 1949–September 1957
## Sunday Afternoons, 1957–61

On a Thursday evening in September 1949, this daring and resourceful masked rider of the plains came thundering onto television and into America's living rooms. Every Thursday for eight years he saved the Old West from more desperadoes than you could imagine — in the process never killing a single one of them — then continued his outlaw fighting on Sunday afternoons for another four years after being dumped from ABC's nighttime schedule. With a total of over 200 episodes produced, many were later edited and made into 90-minute feature films.

Who will ever forget the sight of the Lone Ranger, along with his faithful Indian companion, Tonto, riding across the screen to the strains of Rossini's "William Tell Overture"? Who can forget the solemn tones of the announcer, inviting us to "return to those thrilling days of yesteryear as the Lone Ranger rides again"? That was pretty heady stuff, and excitingly different as well, since in most other Westerns, the Indians and the masked men were the bad guys — yet here they were the good guys! Of course, the Lone Ranger *was* dressed in white, and until the adult Westerns came along, the good guys always wore white and rode a white horse (the sole exception was Hopalong Cassidy, who did wear black). After the adult Westerns made their appearance, a good guy like Wyatt Earp or Paladin might wear black. But "The Lone Ranger" was more for the kids, and in a kid's Western, the good guys wore white.

Despite the show's obvious orientation towards children, adults watched the mysterious masked man too, no doubt feeling the show as one of the more wholesome shoot-'em-ups on the tube, a fact which might garner it a great deal of support today.

Clayton Moore portrayed the daring masked man for all but two years of its network run, with John Hart hiding behind the mask from 1952 to 1954. The faithful Indian companion, Tonto, was played by Jay Silverheels (a mixed-blood Mohawk) the entire time.

Basically, the series was the story of Texas Ranger John Reid, who had been one of six Rangers ambushed by an outlaw gang led by the nefarious Butch Cavendish. While five died, the wounded Reid made it to a water hole, where he was found by Tonto, a childhood friend whose life he had once saved. Nursed back to health, Reid vowed to avenge his fellow Rangers' deaths — with the help, naturally, of Tonto, who called him "kemo sabe" (which supposedly meant "trusty scout"). After the chore of dispatching the Cavendish gang was completed, the duo set out to avenge other wrongs that were being committed wherever they might go. Once a week you could count on the Lone Ranger leaving his trademark — a silver bullet — behind, and someone asking "who was that masked man?" Similarly, you could always anticipate the answer, "why, that's the Lone Ranger," his name being spoken in almost reverential tones.

And once you'd heard that, you could watch the dynamic duo of the West ride off, the masked man calling out to his horse, "Hi Yo Silver," as they rode off to solve someone else's problems.

Appearing first on radio on January 30, 1933, the series aired until May 27, 1955, first on Detroit station WXYZ, then on the Mutual Network and eventually ABC. By the time it made the transition to television, the series was already an American institution, with the Lone Ranger becoming the most respected champion of justice in the Old West. He was a tough man with a will of iron and an unswerving sense of justice. The clean-living Ranger never smoked, drank, or kissed a girl, he never shot to kill, and he subscribed to the highest ideals of the American way of life, retaining his credibility to the end.

Vetern Hollywood actor Moore had portrayed another masked do-gooder, Zorro, in the Saturday morning theatrical serial "Ghost of Zorro." Throughout the time he portrayed the Lone Ranger, Moore adopted a lifestyle similar to that of his character. In interviews, he would refuse to answer questions about topics other than the Lone Ranger, his moralistic attitude, and his impact on the American way of life.

Beside the weekly programs that were later edited into feature films, there were two entirely new movies produced in the late 1950s. In addition, in an attempt to keep the character alive for a while longer, there was a cartoon version in the early 1960s. When a new feature-length Lone Ranger movie was made in the early 1980s with a different actor in the lead, Moore was unmasked, but a court ruled in late 1984 that he still had the right to wear the mask and make personal appearances as the Lone Ranger.

Recorded Theme Music: The "William Tell Overture" has been recorded by numerous orchestras on many record labels.

# The Loner
*CBS, September 1965–April 1966*

After making the oceans safe for humans in the syndicated "Sea Hunt," Lloyd Bridges, like so many others, took a shot at making the

Old West safe. As William Colton, a former Union Cavalry officer during the Civil War, he headed West in search of adventure and the meaning of life. Whether he found it or not, we'll never know.

Despite Bridges being a familiar face to TV viewers, his only previous network series was the anthology series "The Lloyd Bridges Show," which aired on CBS in 1962–63. After "The Loner," he appeared in "San Francisco International Airport" (1970–71) and the police series "Joe Forrester" (1975–76). He also appeared in the epic "Roots" — but didn't everyone?

## A Man Called Shenandoah
*ABC, September 1965–September 1966*

In 1962, Robert Horton left the highly successful ratings winner "Wagon Train," vowing never to do another Western. Unfortunately for him, he found his talents weren't that much in demand, and he soon found himself eating his words and riding the range once more. This time he was in search of his identity. Shot in the desert, he was found and taken to the nearest town by two buffalo hunters, who were hoping he was an outlaw with a price on his head. They soon found out he was just another cowpoke who had been in a gunfight, but who had developed a case of amnesia and for some reason took the name Shenandoah. Not only did he never find out who he was, the series never found an appreciative audience.

## The Man from Blackhawk
*ABC, October 1959–September 1960*

Despite the somewhat unusual twist to this series, it could only manage one year, since it soon became obvious that people weren't all that interested in the exploits of an insurance investigator in the Old West. Robert Rockwell appeared as Sam Logan, the Chicago-based investigator for the Blackhawk Insurance Company. When it became necessary to defend himself, he seldom used a gun, but relied on either his wits or his fists as he traveled from the typical frontier town to cities

Robert Rockwell is probably remembered more for his portrayal of Philip
Boynton on "Our Miss Brooks" from 1952 to 1956 than he is for his role as Sam
Logan, A Chicago-based insurance investigator for the Blackhawk Insurance
Company in "The Man from Blackhawk."

such as San Francisco, settling claims and investigating attempts to
defraud the company.

    If Rockwell looked familiar, it was because his main claim to fame
rested in his portrayal of Eve Arden's would-be love interest Philip
Boynton on "Our Miss Brooks" from 1952 to 1956.

# The Marshal of Gunsight Pass
*ABC, March 1950–September 1950*

You say you don't remember this one? Never heard of it? Along with "The Lone Ranger," it represented one of ABC's first attempts to offer a Western to the viewing public. Unlike the famous Ranger, the marshal didn't hang around for very long. Star Russell "Lucky" Hayden is perhaps best remembered for appearing in a large number of Hopalong Cassidy movies. Roscoe Ates was his sidekick, who could be counted upon to provide comic relief.

# Maverick
*ABC, September 1957–September 1961*

In most Westerns, cowboys spent their time chasing the bad guys, fighting off the seemingly ever-present hostile Indians, or rounding up cattle. But the Maverick brothers, Bret (James Garner, 1957–60), Bart (Jack Kelly), Cousin Beauregard (Roger Moore, 1960–61), and Brent (Robert Colbert, 1961), represented an entirely different breed, preferring to spend their time playing poker at the card tables or using one of the back roads out of town if the possibility of a gunfight loomed. Bret, as a matter of fact, would never win a fast-draw contest, and only Beau, who replaced Garner for one season, could ever claim to have been a fighter.

Originally conceived and introduced as a regular Western dealing with the adventures and exploits of a card sharp, the series took a humorous turn when Garner elected to play a scene for laughs. Soon, the entire series was being played in that direction, despite the introduction of brother Bart in November 1957, whose sole purpose, it seemed, was to keep the series on the straight and narrow. Although the tone was humorous, the series was definitely a regular Western.

In 1960, in what amounted to a rerun of the Clint Walker feud between Warner Brothers and the series star, Garner departed, insisting he be given a better contract. In keeping with their policy of not giving in to their stars, Warners once more hired a replacement, this time in the form of Cousin Beau, who had moved to England following the Civil War and who was now a refined Englishman.

Cousin Beau and Brother Bart swapped leads for the entire 1960–61 season after a court ruled that Garner could not be held to his

*Left:* James Garner went on to become one of the biggest stars in Hollywood, but he got his start as Bret Maverick, playing that role from 1957 to 1960. An attempt to reprise the series in the early 1980s with Garner in the same role failed miserably, but by that time he had established himself as a major star on both television and in the movies. His "The Rockford Files," a tongue-in-cheek detective series, ran for a number of years, beginning in 1974. Two years earlier, he had attempted a return in Westerns in "Nichols," a one-year wonder in which he was killed and then returned, playing his twin brother. *Right:* Jack Kelly was Maverick brother Bart, the only one to be with the series the entire time it was on the air. Following the demise of "Maverick," he acted as host for the "NBC Comedy Playhouse" in 1970 and "NBC Comedy Theater" in 1971–72.

contract. At that time, still another brother, Brent, entered the scene and took over the lead in the series in early 1961. By the fall of 1961, it was quite obvious Garner was the true star of the series, and when Bart wasn't seen alone in new episodes, repeats were shown of earlier episodes which featured Garner.

Garner, after failing to ride the range again in the short-lived

"Nichols" in 1971–72, moved to contemporary drama, portraying private detective James Rockford in the highly successful tongue-in-cheek "The Rockford Files" which began in 1974. An attempt to revive Bret in the early 1980s and to capitalize on Garner's popularity resulted in the series "Bret Maverick," which was cancelled shortly after it began. The pilot movie for the series was highly successful, but despite Garner's popularity and appeal, the series never took off.

Kelly, meanwhile, wrapped up his television acting career (apart from occasional guest shots) as the host for "NBC Comedy Playhouse" in 1970 and "NBC Comedy Theater" in 1971–72.

Moore portrayed super-sleuth Simon Templer in the mystery series "The Saint" from 1967 to 1969 and starred in "The Persuaders" in 1971–72, but it is as Secret Agent 007 of the James Bond movies that Moore is best known.

Recorded Theme Music: "Maverick," the Sons of the Pioneers, RCA Children's Bluebird Records.

# The Men from Shiloh

See "The Virginian." Same program, different title in its final year.

# The Monroes
### *ABC, September 1966–August 1967*

Like the later "Little House on the Prairie" and "The Waltons," this series tended to present family living at its best under trying circumstances. In other words, basically pretty tame stuff. The series presented the story of five orphaned youngsters, aged 6 to 18, trying to put down roots (via the homestead route) in the Wyoming Territory in 1876. The obligatory villain was the dastardly British cattle baron Major Mapoy, fiendishly portrayed by Liam Sullivan. The equally obligatory renegade Indian who was really a good guy—just misunderstood—was Dirty Jim, played by Ron Soble. The heads of the family were 18-year-old Clayt (Michael Anderson, Jr.) and 16-year-old Kathy (Barbara Hershey), who had their hands full controlling the 13-year-old twins, Jefferson and Fennimore (Keith and Kevin Schultz), and 6-year-old Amy (Tammy Locke). Also appearing were Jim

Westmoreland as Ruel Jaxon, one of Mapoy's cowhands, Ben Johnson as Sleeve, and Robert Middleton as Barney Wales.

# The New Land
### *ABC, September 1974–October 1974*

A quasi–"Little House on the Prairie," this series definitely did not have the staying power of the Michael Landon series (which seemingly ran forever) that began the same month. But for six weeks, the handful of viewers who watched saw the Larsen family, Anna (Bonnie Bedelia) and Christian (Scott Thomas), along with their children Tuliff (Todd Lookinland) and Annaliese (Debbie Lytton) and best friend Bo (Kurt Russell) attempt to carve out a life near Selna, Minnesota, right on the edge of the West, in 1858.

# Nichols
### *NBC, September 1971–August 1972*

Make no mistake about it, James Garner is a fine actor. However, he apparently hasn't decided whether he wants to be remembered as a serious actor or a comedian, so he's made a career of combining the two. In the movies, it seems to work, but on Westerns you couldn't always pull it off, as he soon found out. In the tongue-in-cheek "Maverick," he was always concocting a get rich(er) quick scheme; in the reincarnation of that series in the early 1980s, things hadn't changed much and "Nichols," which fell between Maverick I and Maverick II, was essentially a reworking of the same old plots.

There were some twists, however. In "Nichols," Garner returned to Nichols, Arizona, the town his family had founded in 1914. Nichols, instead of riding a horse, rode around in an early twentieth century car or on an early version of a motorcycle, although he could be found on horseback occasionally. Like Maverick, he hated violence. To top it all off, he got killed at the end and was replaced by his twin brother Jim Nichols, also played by you-know-who.

Besides attempting to find the ultimate get-rich-quick scheme, Nichols (no first name, just Nichols) was blackmailed by the villainous Ma Ketcham (Neva Patterson) into serving as sheriff so she could keep her eye on him. While Nichols had been busy spending 18 years in the army, the Ketcham clan had proceeded to take over the town, so the position of sheriff was naturally powerless — just the way Nichols liked it.

Mitch (Stuart Margolin) was the town bully, not to mention being Ma's son and Nichols' deputy; Ruth (Margot Kidder), the barmaid, was Nichols' lady friend; and Bertha (Alice Ghostley) owned the saloon.

And why was Nichols shot and killed, you ask? Low ratings. But it didn't do any good, since the show had been consigned to oblivion by the time the killing episode aired.

Kidder, meanwhile, was to go on to bigger and better things in the movies and perhaps is best remembered for her portrayal of Lois Lane in the *Superman* film series. Margolin and Garner would get together again in a couple of years in "The Rockford Files," which next to "Maverick" was Garner's most successful series.

# The Nine Lives of Elfego Baca

Another Disney entry, appearing sporadically under the "Frontierland" banner on the Walt Disney series, this one aired in 1958 and marked the studio's first true attempt at moving from frontiersmen to the Old West. Robert Loggia portrayed the peace-loving Baca, who was a lawman in Tombstone, Arizona. All in all, it was pretty much your standard Western fare.

## Northwest Passage
### NBC, September 1958–September 1959

Proving that there was life after "Davy Crockett" and before Jed Clampett and "Barnaby Jones," Buddy Ebsen popped up on this drama about the French and Indian War as Sgt. Hunk Marriner, faithful companion and erstwhile sidekick of Major Robert Rogers (Keith Larsen). Rogers, an experienced Indian fighter, had organized Rogers' Rangers to help him search for an inland waterway that would allow boat traffic to cross the breadth of America. Another companion was Ensign Langdon Towne (Don Burnett), a well-to-do Harvard graduate who was the company mapmaker. Although they never found the Northwest Passage, they did find the time to do a great deal of fighting with the French and the Indians in eastern Canada and upstate New York, making this the most eastern of Westerns (of course, in the time period in which this series was set, the Wild West was Indiana).

# The Oregon Trail
## NBC, September 1977–October 1977

You couldn't make much distance in a wagon train over a period of six weeks, and this series didn't either. It was 1842, and Evan Thorpe, portrayed by the Australian-born Rod Taylor, was a widower who had decided to pack up his belongings and three kids, Andy (Andrew Stevens), William (Tony Becker), and Rachel (Gina Marie Smika), and start over again in the Oregon Territory. When the original leader of the wagon train he had joined proved to be unreliable, Thorpe was elected to serve as the leader. Naturally, between fighting off unfriendly Indians and battling the elements, he found the time to develop a romantic interest in Margaret Devlin (Darleen Carr), who also just happened to be alone. Luther Sprague (Charles Napier) was the standard old scout.

# The Outcasts
## ABC, September 1968–September 1969

The only Western with a black leading character, this violence-filled series featured Don Murray as Earl Corey, a Virginia aristocrat who had become a gunman and drifter, and Otis Young as Jemal David, a freed slave who had become a bounty hunter.

In the years following the Civil War, the two pursued their common goal of tracking down wanted criminals and, of course, making money, with their backgrounds providing a less-than-stable basis for their tenuous relationship.

# The Outlaws
## NBC, September 1960–September 1962

As originally presented, the series took a novel approach to the good guys vs. bad guys problem, looking at the battle between the lawmen and the desperadoes through the eyes of the latter. But by its second year, all but one of the original cast had either ridden off into the sunset or had bitten the dust and been replaced, and the series' emphasis shifted to the standard "through the eyes of the lawman" focus.

For the first season, the show was set in the Oklahoma Territory in the 1890s and followed the adventures and activities of United States Marshal Frank Caine (Barton MacLane) and his deputies, Will Forman (Don Collier) and Heck Martin (Jock Gaynor).

In its second season, the marshals found themselves headquartered in Stillwater, Oklahoma; Forman had become a marshal, with Chalk Breeson (Bruce Yarnell) serving as his deputy. Also added to the cast was Connie Masters (Judy Lewis), who worked at the Wells Fargo office, and Slim (Slim Pickens), who could always be counted upon to wind up in a predicament of some sort, supplying limited comic relief.

# The Overland Trail
## NBC, February 1960–September 1960

Proving there was some life after appearing as Chester A. Riley on "The Life of Riley" from 1953 to 1958, the late William Bendix took a fling at the cowboy trail. He appeared as Frederick Thomas Kelly, a former civil engineer and Union Army guerilla who, along with his sidekick Frank Flippen (Doug McClure), was in charge of moving a stage line from Missouri to the Pacific. As could be expected, the adventures of their passengers, not to mention their own, provided the stories. Sadly, they never made it to the Pacific.

# Pall Mall Playhouse
## ABC, July 1955–September 1955

If you ever wondered what happened to unsold Western pilots starring such people as Will Rogers, Jr., and John Ireland, some of them wound up on this summertime replacement series.

# The Quest
*NBC, September 1976–December 1976*

During the 1890s, two young brothers, Morgan Beaudine (Kurt Russell) and Quentin Beaudine (Tim Matheson), traversed the Old West in search of their sister, who had been kidnapped by the Cheyenne Indians. Morgan had also been kidnapped, but the pair had become separated. Morgan, although now living in the white man's world, thought of himself more as an Indian, wore Indian dress, and even had an Indian name, Two Persons. Brother Quentin, on the other hand, planned to become a doctor and had been educated in San Francisco. Sadly, they never found their sister, nor did the series find enough ratings to keep it around for more than a few months.

# The Range Rider
*Syndicated*

Before he grew a mustache and became Yancy Derringer, Jock Mahoney was the Range Rider, a Wild Bill Hickok clone, complete with fringed buckskin jacket. Dick West was played by Dick Jones, who was later to pop up in "Buffalo Bill, Jr." and was the obligatory sidekick.

# Rawhide
*CBS, January 1959–January 1966*

What can you possibly say that is bad about a program that served to introduce Clint Eastwood to the American public? Although he never once uttered a line so profound and memorable as "go ahead, make my day," the show made him a star, and the spaghetti Westerns he made in Italy after the series finished its run only tended to increase his fame. He parlayed that success into a series of police dramas as "Dirty Harry" Callahan, and he remains an enormous box-office draw despite several recent less-than-successful film ventures. Ironically, although Eastwood was to become the biggest star, the series was originally designed as a vehicle for veteran movie actor Eric Fleming, whose only other TV exposure was in the World War II series "The Flying Tigers" on the DuMont Network in 1951. Fleming portrayed trail boss Gil Favor, but it was Eastwood's portrayal of Rowdy Yates the public remembers.

In addition to Eastwood, two others, Paul Brinegar (as Wishbone, the cook) and Steve Raines (as Jim Quince) rode the range throughout the seven years of the series' run. Others appearing in the series included country singer Sheb Wooley (as Pete Nolan, 1959–65); Rocky Shahan (as Joe Scarlett, 1959–64); James Murdock (as Mushy, 1959–65); Robert Cabal (as Jesus Patines, 1961–64); Charles Gray (as Clay Forrester, 1962–63); David Watson (as Ian Cabot, 1965–66); and Raymond St. Jacques (as Solomon King, 1965–66).

Wooley had recorded the million-selling novelty record "Purple People Eater" in 1958. Eastwood also took a shot at a recording career. His initial effort, "Cowboy Wedding Song" on Cameo Records, issued while the series was still on the air, is considered quite valuable and rare. Close to 20 years later, he recorded again with Merle Haggard, T.G. Shepard, and Ray Charles, and this time the records were substantial hits, although the records were less Eastwood's than they were the other artists'. It's unlikely that any other Western series featured two performers with a number of records under their belts (Wooley continued his career well into the 1970s with novelty country records under the name of Ben Colder).

Basically, "Rawhide" was your standard Western fare and featured stories which had no doubt been told in the movies countless times before: Cattle drovers had a herd of cattle they had to get from one point to another, and their adventures and misadventures along the way provided fuel for the scripts. Those scripts usually involved Indians, would-be rustlers, cattle stampedes, or run-ins with someone they had known before. Toward the end of the last drive, Fleming drowned while on location for a movie filming in South America. Eastwood took over as trail boss, and although the theme song may have urged him to "keep them dogies rollin'," by then the show was ready to go to that last great roundup.

Recorded Theme Music: "Rawhide," Frankie Laine, Columbia Records.

# The Rebel
*ABC, October 1959–September 1961*

The late Nick Adams was Johnny Yuma, a former Confederate soldier who traveled from town to town in the years following the Civil

War. Fed up with violence after the war, he often found himself the go-between in both criminal and moral issues.

After being cancelled by ABC, the series was rerun during the summer of 1962 on NBC.

Recorded Theme Music: "The Rebel," Johnny Cash, Columbia Records.

# Redigo
### NBC, September 1963–December 1963

Although "Empire" had failed the preceding season, the powers that be at NBC had enough faith in the central character, Jim Redigo (Richard Egan), that they gave him his own series. They shouldn't have wasted their time; "Redigo" lasted an even shorter period of time than its predecessor. Instead of managing a large ranch in the contemporary Southwest, Redigo was now the owner of his own small spread, and the stories revolved around his attempts to make a profit and the relationships he encountered. Mike (Roger Davis) and Frank Martinez (Rudy Solari) were the most prominent ranch hands, while the romantic interest was provided by Gerry (Elena Verdugo), who managed a nearby hotel.

Verdugo fared much better a few years later when she appeared as Consuelo Lopez in the long-running medical drama "Marcus Welby, M.D." with Robert Young. She was also featured in the 1964–65 sitcom "Many Happy Returns," and in "Mona McCluskey" in 1965–66, but she may be best remembered by early TV viewers as the star of "Meet Millie," which ran from 1952 to 1956.

Davis wasn't quite through with the West, winding up on "Alias Smith and Jones" following Pete Duel's death.

# The Restless Gun
### NBC, September 1957–September 1959

Veteran actor John Payne portrayed Vint Bonner, a peace-loving loner who used violence to solve problems only as a last resort. Often he found that violence was thrust upon him because he was acknowledged as the fastest gun in the West, a reputation that followed him everywhere he went. He wanted little more than to settle down somewhere, but few towns wanted a notorious gunslinger among their citizens, and he was forced to work as a ranch hand, cattle drover, Indian scout, or whatever else he might be able to find.

Payne, who had served in the Army Air Corps during World War II, would seem an unlikely choice for a cowboy hero, having starred with Betty Grable in several musicals while under contract to 20th Century–Fox.

Like so many other series, the pilot episode for this one was shown on another program, in this case "The Schlitz Playhouse of Stars," a series which served to introduce several Western characters to television audiences.

Recorded Theme Music: "The Restless Gun," Sons of the Pioneers, RCA Children's Bluebird Records.

# The Rifleman
### ABC, September 1958–July 1963

Chuck Connors had a two-year major league baseball career in 1949 and 1951 with the Brooklyn Dodgers and Chicago Cubs. At best his stint in the majors could be called mediocre; he appeared in a total of 67 games with a career batting average of .238. So the former first baseman traded in his bat and glove for a fling at Hollywood, where he had become well known playing in the Pacific Coast League for several years. That career proved to be much more successful, since he appeared in four other series in addition to "The Rifleman," the one for which he is easily best remembered.

While none of his later attempts in a starring role had the staying power of this one, for five years Connors, as Lucas McCain, helped maintain law and order in North Fork, New Mexico, even though he was just a widower and homesteader who was trying to eke out a living while raising his motherless son, Mark (Johnny Crawford).

Unfortunately—or fortunately, depending upon your point of view—the marshal, Micah Torrance (Paul Fix) was somewhat inept when it came to fending off the desperadoes who came riding into North Fork on an almost weekly basis. As might be expected, when the bad guys showed up he had to turn to Lucas for help. With the aid of his trusty trick rifle, a modified Winchester with a large ring that cocked the hammer as he drew, McCain could be counted upon either to eliminate the bad guys or to send them running out of town.

*Left*: Hollywood veteran John Payne portrayed Vint Bonner in NBC's "The Restless Gun" for several years in the late 1950s. The series wasn't spectacular by any stretch of the imagination, but it was enjoyable. *Right*: Chuck Connors is probably better remembered for his role as Lucas McCain in "The Rifleman," which ran from 1958 to 1963, than for "Branded," "Cowboy in Africa," or the police/courtroom drama "Arrest and Trial." Among sports fans, particularly Brooklyn Dodgers and Chicago Cubs fans, he may be remembered as a so-so player in the early 1950s.

After suffering through several years of Lucas' increasingly moralistic tones, viewers became fed up with the series. In an attempt to salvage the ratings, Lucas was given a love interest in 1962 in the person of Miss Molly Scott (Joan Taylor), North Fork's resident storekeeper. In the series' final year, Patricia Blair arrived on the scene as Lou Mallory, a con artist who really wasn't all that bad even though she was attempting to buy up as much land as possible when she wasn't running the local hotel.

For Crawford, the series served as a springboard to a successful acting and recording career; he had a number of teenage-oriented hit
records during the series' run, the biggest of which was "Cindy's Birth-
day" in 1962. He and his brother Bobby, who was featured on
"Laramie" for several years, also recorded several records as the
Crawford Brothers, but none of those made any impact on the charts.

# Riverboat
*NBC, September 1959–January 1961*

Say what you will about this series, but it was for Burt Reynolds
what "Rawhide" was for Clint Eastwood, a jumping-off point for
future superstardom. Unlike Eastwood, who rode the range for eight
years, Reynolds floated up and down the Mississippi River for only half
the series' first season, but everybody has to start someplace. For
Reynolds, television tended to offer steady employment: He popped
up on "Gunsmoke" several years later, then moved on to star in two
other series, both of them detective dramas, "Dan August" and
"Hawk." A pilot for a third, "Lassiter," wasn't picked up by any of the
networks. Shortly after that he became America's "good-old-boy" in
residence, starring in such movies as *Smokey and the Bandit*. He remains a major box office draw.
    Undeniably, "Riverboat" was a starring vehicle for Darren
McGavin (Grey Holden), who had just completed a run in syndication
in the original TV version of "Mickey Spillane's Mike Hammer." Earlier
he had appeared in "Crime Photographer" (1951–52), and he was later
to wind up as a private eye in "The Outsider" and as a newspaper
reporter in the cult favorite occult series "Kolchak: The Night Stalker."
    According to the "Riverboat" storyline, Holden was the captain
and owner of the *Enterprise*, a 100-foot-long paddlewheeler, during
the 1840s. After winning the boat in a poker game, he was determined
to turn a profit in any way possible, but profits tended to be few and
far between. Reynolds (Ben Frazer) was the co-star at the beginning,
but by the middle of that first year, both he and crew member Travis
(William D. Gordon) found themselves adrift.
    Returning for his second season, McGavin had a new co-star in
Noah Beery, who portrayed Bill Blake. Blake had purchased 49 percent
of the boat and spent much of his time figuring out ways to take con-
trol, an endeavor which proved unsuccessful by the time the *Enterprise*

sailed off into oblivion. In addition, during that second season, Holden spent more time away from the boat and more time with the ladies than he did during the first season.

## The Road West
### NBC, September 1966–August 1967

Another family-oriented Western, this one concerned the trials and tribulations of Benjamin Pride (Barry Sullivan) and his family in the Kansas Territory after the Civil War. Pride, a widower, had married Elizabeth Reynolds (Kathryn Hays) prior to uprooting the family from their Springfield, Ohio, home. Naturally, her brother, Chance (Glenn Corbett), decided to tag along in search of adventure and excitement.

Also appearing were Andrew Prine as Benjamin's 24-year-old son, Timothy, Brenda Scott as his 18-year-old daughter, Midge, and Kelly Corcoran as 8-year-old Kip. Also joining in on the family's move westward was Grandpa Pride (Charles Seel).

## The Rough Riders
### ABC, October 1958–September 1959

The Civil War ended in 1865, and with its end the westward migration resumed in earnest. Jim Flagg (Kent Taylor) and Buck Sinclair (Peter Whitney) had served in the Union Army, while their traveling companion, Lt. Kirby (Jan Merlin), had been in the Confederate Army. Along the way, they encountered the expected Indians, outlaws, and other bad guys.

Merlin, a true television pioneer, had appeared on the classic children's series "Tom Corbett, Space Cadet" as Roger Manning from 1950 to 1952. This series quickly brought him down to earth.

## The Roy Rogers Show
### NBC, December 1951–June 1957

Not to be confused with the short-lived "Roy Rogers and Dale Evans" variety show, which aired for three months in 1962, this mostly

Roy Rogers, "King of the Cowboys." Along with his wife, trail mate, and sing-ing partner, Dale Evans, Rogers sang his way from a successful radio show of the 1940s and 1950s to a smash television hit that lasted five and one half years.

contemporary Western hung around for a total of five and one half years following essentially the same formula as Gene Autry. In fact, much of Rogers' career was spent in the shadow of Autry, but that didn't seem to bother Rogers, who became a major star in his own right.

Autry was the first of the singing cowboys, and Rogers was the sec-ond. Like Autry, Rogers parlayed his success on the screen into a suc-cessful recording career, although he achieved nowhere near the success of his counterpart. But don't go feeling sorry for Roy; you won't find him standing in the bread lines anytime soon.

Born Leonard Slye in Duck Run, Ohio, a suburb of Portsmouth which no longer exists, Rogers followed the Okie migration westward in the mid-1930s. He started a singing career with Uncle Tom Murray's Hollywood Hillbillies in 1931 and moved on to become a member of the Sons of the Pioneers a few years later. But it was as a solo star that Rogers made his mark, his recording of "Here Comes Peter Cottontail" being one of the biggest Easter songs of all time, ranking behind Irving Berlin's "Easter Parade."

Rogers made over 80 films, all for Republic Pictures, the same studio which featured Autry. He received his big break in 1937 when he auditioned and was chosen to take over as Republic's cowboy star-in-residence when Autry left the studio following an argument with the boss. Earlier, Rogers had appeared in several minor supporting roles in Westerns, but this represented his best opportunity, and he took advantage of the situation. A radio career was to follow in 1944, with his show featuring different personalities but following the successful pattern laid down by Autry.

Rogers' first wife, Arlene, died in 1946. By that time he and Dale Evans had teamed up as the king and queen of the Old West, and so they made it official, tying the knot on December 31, 1947. The following year, the Sons of the Pioneers (who had become major recording stars in their own right) and Rogers parted company. Pat Brady then became Rogers' sidekick in a relationship that was to last through both the radio and TV series.

The radio series closed up shop in 1955 after 11 years on the air, leaving Roy, Dale, and Pat free to concentrate on the TV series, which still had several years to run.

In the interim, the "King of the Cowboys" had become the most popular of the cowboys on television—at least with the kids toward whom the show was geared. Unfortunately for Roy and Dale, the kids didn't have much to say about the Nielsen ratings, and once the "adult Westerns" appeared, it was only a matter of time before the duo was consigned to oblivion.

Roy was joined every week at the Double R Bar Ranch by Dale, Pat (and Pat's jeep, Nellybelle), Trigger the wonder horse, and Bullet the German Shepherd in righting the usual wrongs one might expect such a heroic figure to encounter. Like Autry's sidekick, Pat Buttram, Brady could be expected each week to get into an unusual predicament from which Rogers would have to extricate him. Naturally, Trigger would have the opportunity to perform a trick or two as well. And, like

Autry, Roy and/or Dale could always find time for a song somewhere along the way. It was pretty tame stuff, but the kids loved it.

Recorded Theme Music: "Happy Trails (to You)," Roy and Dale, RCA Victor Records and RCA Bluebird Children's Records.

Other Music of Interest: The Sons of the Pioneers, both with and without Rogers, had numerous singles and albums on RCA Victor and the company's budget label, RCA Camden.

# The Saga of Andy Burnette

Another Disney multi-parter appearing under the "Frontierland" banner, this show was based on the book *Andy Burnette's Diary* and aired in 1958. In fact, there was a real Andy Burnette, just as there was a real Davy Crockett, but it is highly unlikely he looked anything like Jerome Courtland, the series' clean-shaven star. Disney's Burnette was a young frontiersman who had aspirations of becoming a full-fledged mountain man. The series revolved around his adventures in the Wyoming/Colorado/Dakotas area, circa 1830–40. One week Burnette might attempt to join up with a crew of buffalo hunters; the next week he might be scouting for the army, all the while manning his traps and searching for his own private place in the Rockies.

Recorded Theme Music: "The Saga of Andy Burnette," Jerome Courtland, Mickey Mouse Club Records.

# Sara
## *CBS, February 1976–July 1976*

Take a strong-willed schoolteacher, place her in Independence, Colorado, in the 1870s, throw in a few battles with the townspeople (who had expected a more-or-less stodgy type), and you have the basic plot of this short-lived series.

Brenda Vaccaro was Sara Yarnell, a teacher who had moved West for the challenges it presented. She wasn't prepared, however, to battle most of the townspeople, who did not want a teacher who was outspoken. Emmet Ferguson (Bert Kramer), Claude Barstow (William Phipps), and George Bailey (William Wintersole) were the school board members who didn't quite know what to make of her. Her allies were newspaper editor Martin Pope (Albert Stratton) and her friend

"The Saga of Andy Burnette," a Walt Disney miniseries that aired in 1958, featured Jerome Courtland in the role of the real-life mountain man and frontiersman. The series marked the end of Courtland's involvement with television in front of the cameras; in recent years he has been behind them, as a director.

Julia Bailey (Mariclare Costello), and her adamant foe was her landlady, Martha Higgins (Louise Latham), who felt that teachers should teach in a conventional style and keep their mouths shut.

## Saturday Roundup
### NBC, June 1951–September 1951

Kermit Maynard, the younger brother of legendary cowboy star Ken Maynard, starred in one of NBC's first attempts at a Western, an anthology series dramatizing the stories of James Oliver Curwood. Maynard's character varied from week to week. His previous claim to fame was that he was a former world champion rodeo rider who appeared in numerous "B" Westerns during the 1930s. He obviously never achieved the legendary status accorded his brother.

## Sergeant Preston of the Yukon
*CBS, September 1955–September 1958*

For three years every Thursday night you could count on this Mountie always getting his man, just like members of the Royal Canadian Mounted Police are supposed to do. The show was centered not in the Old West, but rather in the Old Klondike around the end of the nineteenth century. Sgt. Preston almost single-handedly made the Yukon a safer place to live—assuming anyone would want to live there.

Aided by his faithful dog, Yukon King, and his horse, Rex, Preston (Richard Simmons, not to be confused with the exercise guru of the same name) eliminated the bad guys who were trying to take advantage of the gold prospectors during the Gold Rush.

Strictly a kid's series, the show was based on the radio series of the same name, which made its debut on ABC Radio on June 12, 1947, under its original title, "The Challenge of the Yukon." That title was changed six years later to include the lead character, which obviously made things easier for the TV executives; at least they wouldn't have to change the title midway through the series' run. And, when the radio series left the air in 1955, it promptly became a television series.

At times, it was difficult to tell who was the real star of the show, Yukon King or Sgt. Preston, since the dog figured prominently in the story lines, constantly mauling crooks and bushwhackers, chewing guns out of their grubby hands, and hauling down one villain after another with the erstwhile Sgt. Preston finishing off the others.

Unlike other series, most of which saw fit to use fake snow, this series was filmed outdoors in the real snow to lend an air of authenticity (although the snow was in the mountains of California and Colorado instead of Canada).

# Shane
*ABC, September 1966–December 1966*

The cry of "Shane, come back" by young Brandon de Wilde in the movie *Shane* is one of the most poignant in film history. Unfortunately, the series with the same name was anything but poignant. Like most other movies that were adapted to television series, this one laid an egg, lasting a mere three months—and no one cried out for it to come back.

Some time before he was to reach stardom as Caine on "Kung Fu," David Carradine appeared as Shane, a wandering gunfighter. He stopped off at the ranch of the recently widowed Marian Starett (Jill Ireland) and found her encountering the usual difficulties protecting her homestead against nature and the vicious Rufe Ryker (Bert Freed), who claimed the land was his.

Christopher Shea was Marian's eight-year-old son, Joey; Tom Tully, her father-in-law; and Sam Gilman was Sam Grafton, the saloon owner.

# The Sheriff of Cochise
*Syndicated*

Obviously, it was set in Arizona. Cochise County to be exact. The series was also known as "U.S. Marshal," and need more be said? John Bromfield starred in a contemporary setting.

# Shotgun Slade
*Syndicated*

A typical Western featuring movie veteran Scott Brady as Slade.

# Sky King
*ABC, September 1953–September 1954*

If your memory tells you this series lasted longer than one year, it's correct. It lasted three years (featuring new episodes), from 1951 to 1954, but only one of those seasons was in prime time. What the kids liked on Saturday and Sunday mornings and afternoons didn't fare too well in the evening when Mom and Pop controlled the tube. From 1959 to 1966, Sky King showed up again on Saturday afternoons, with the intrepid flyboy fighting the bad guys for more than 11 years.

Billed as "America's favorite flying cowboy" (not to mention the only one) for eight years on radio from October 28, 1946, until 1954, Sky King proved to be somewhat more popular on television. The late Kirby Grant was Sky King, a rancher who just happened to be a pilot. He could be counted upon to get the best of the bad guys using his twin-engine Cessna, the *Songbird*, instead of a horse to get from his Arizona-based Flying Crown Ranch to wherever he was needed.

He was aided in his exploits by his teenage niece, Penny (Gloria Winters), and nephew, Clipper (Ron Haggerty).

By the time the series made its debut, Winters was already a TV veteran, appearing as Chester A. Riley's daughter, Babs, in the Jackie Gleason version of "The Life of Riley" in 1949–50.

# Stagecoach West
### ABC, October 1960–September 1961

If imitation is the sincerest form of flattery, the producers of "Wagon Train" had to be the most flattered people around when this series hit the air, since it was, in effect, "Wagon Train" with the covered wagons replaced by a stagecoach.

Wayne Rogers — who would go on to much better things when he portrayed Trapper John McIntyre on the TV version of "M.A.S.H." from 1972 to 1975 — was Luke Perry, Robert Bray was Simon Kane, and Richard Eyer was his son, David, who just happened to be along for the ride, taking up space that could have been used by a paying passenger. As in "Wagon Train," the passengers, the happenings along the way, and the people with whom they came into contact while driving the stagecoaches from Missouri to California provided the basis for the stories.

# Stoney Burke
### ABC, October 1962–September 1963

Before he moved to Hawaii and became Detective Steve McGarrett on "Hawaii Five-O" in 1968 (uttering such memorable lines as,

"Book 'em, Dan-o"), Jack Lord was professional rodeo rider Stoney Burke, whose main goal in life was to win the coveted Golden Buckle, the award given to the world champion saddle bronc rider. Burke's fellow rodeo pals in this contemporary Western included Cody Bristol (Robert Dowdell), E.J. Stocker (Bruce Dern), Ves Painter (Warren Oates), and Red (Bill Hart). Incidentally, he never did win the buckle.

# Sugarfoot
## ABC, September 1957–July 1961

Although it covered a span of four years, this series alternated with several other programs; taking into consideration the number of episodes filmed and aired, the series was actually on the air for a total of only about three years.

Will Hutchins was Tom Brewster, a relatively inept cowboy, hence the "Sugarfoot" appellation. He was also a correspondence-school law student who was searching for adventure and employment while drifting from town to town. Mostly he found trouble and usually a pretty girl. Supposedly he even cracked the books once in a while.

Despite his ineptness as a cowboy, he still managed to capture his share of outlaws in what could best be called a typical Western, with one qualification: Like "Maverick," which came from the same studio, (Warner Bros.), "Sugarfoot" was played with a sense of humor.

Prior to assuming the role in "Sugarfoot," Hutchins was a relative unknown and could hardly have been termed a screen veteran, having appeared in only five television dramas and one movie, *Lafayette Escadrille*, which starred Tab Hunter.

Born Marshall Lowell Hutchason, he had graduated from Pomona College in 1952, was promptly drafted, and served as a cryptographer with the signal corps until his discharge from the army in 1954. He then entered U.C.L.A. to work on his master's degree in motion picture production and was discovered when he auditioned for a bit part in a TV drama.

With a secret desire to be either a boxer or a comedian, Hutchins received his opportunity to try the latter when he starred in the 1966–67 sitcom "Hey Landlord" and again the following year when he portrayed Dagwood Bumstead in "Blondie." He hasn't been heard from since.

From 1957 to 1959, "Sugarfoot" ran on alternate weeks with

He was born Marshall Lowell Hutchason on May 5, 1932, in Los Angeles, the son of a dentist, but those who remember him as Tom Brewster in "Sugarfoot" also recall his stage name, Will Hutchins. A devotee of jazz who listed Louis Armstrong as his favorite musician in a Warner Bros. handout from the 1950s, Hutchins had a secret ambition to be a professional boxer.

"Cheyenne"; with "Bronco" in 1959–60; and during its final year it was one of three alternating series under the "Cheyenne" banner.

Recorded Theme Music: "Sugarfoot," the Sons of the Pioneers, RCA Children's Bluebird Records.

# The Swamp Fox

A short-term Disney miniseries appearing under the "Frontierland" banner in which Leslie Nielson starred as Francis Marion, the Revolutionary War hero. For several weeks on the air he bedeviled those nasty British Redcoats in and around the Charleston, South Carolina, area.

Recorded Theme Music: "Swamp Fox and Six Other Revolutionary War Songs," Disneyland Records. Artists' name(s) not listed on record or on sleeve.

# Tales of the Texas Rangers
### CBS, 1955–58 (Afternoons)
### ABC, December 1958–May 1959

It was seldom that a program could make the switch from being more or less a kids-only daytime show to an adult prime-time show. This one did—or at least it made the valiant attempt, being much more successful in its attempts to teach the kids the history of the famed Texas Rangers than it was in earning high Nielsen ratings.

Starring Willard Parker (Ranger Jace Pearson) and Harry Lauter (Ranger Clay Morgan), the series would jump back and forth from the Old West to the present from one week to the next. While the Rangers had long (about 120 years) been the most famous law enforcement agency in the nation, covering the over 260,000 square miles of Texas, neither Pearson, Morgan, nor their band of 50 men could capture the viewers' attention. Originally, the series was heard on NBC radio beginning on July 8, 1950. It ran for two years, with Joel McCrea playing the part of Pearson.

Recorded Theme Music: "Tales of the Texas Rangers," Shorty Long, RCA Children's Bluebird Records.

# Tales of the West
### Syndicated

Before he became famous as Jock Ewing on the soap opera "Dallas," Jim Davis had compiled a list of credits as a character actor in

"Tales of the Texas Rangers" began on radio and moved over to the small screen a few years later. Willard Parker (left center) was Jace Pearson and Harry Lauter (right center) was Ranger Clay Morgan. The theme song said the Rangers were a band of sturdy men, but from the looks of some of them, you have to wonder. A total of about 50 Rangers covered Texas, if you believed the series.

enough movies and TV series to become one of those faces you not only recognized, but could name when he appeared on your favorite program, which was bound to happen. Prior to "Dallas," this late-fifties series, a spin-off from the 1957 Republic picture *Last Stagecoach West*, represented his sole opportunity to make the best of a starring role.

Each week Davis, who portrayed railroad detective Bill Cameron would set out to apprehend a famous desperado. In the course of the series production, Davis and his cohorts captured such outlaws as Jesse James, Billy the Kid, Butch Cassidy, and just about every other authentic outlaw every school kid had heard of at one time or another. Obviously, numerous liberties were taken with the historical facts, but Davis' abilities as an actor had a tendency to override the scripts, and the show was a cut above your average Western.

# Tales of Wells Fargo
### NBC, March 1957–September 1962

During the course of its eight-year run from 1951 to 1959, the "Schlitz Playhouse of Stars" developed a reputation for offering television viewers the opportunity to see major Hollywood stars such as James Deàn, whom they wouldn't have ordinarily expected to see on the small screen. On numerous instances, some of the plays presented turned out to be pilot films for series. "Tales of Wells Fargo," like "The Restless Gun," was one of the latter.

In the ensuing five years, native Oklahoman Dale Robertson appeared as Jim Hardie. A troubleshooter for the Wells Fargo stage line, he kept the desperadoes and Indians at bay while seeing that the cargo and passengers arrived at their destination safely. The athletic Robertson was well suited for the part; he was voted the Most Outstanding Athlete in his college, starring in football, basketball, and baseball. A former lieutenant in the combat engineers, he brought a certain toughness to the role as well, which made his portrayal, at the very least, seem more realistic.

Wells Fargo was the first, and for a while, the only express company linking the East and the West; in 1857 alone, it transported $60 million in gold. To maintain that function of linking the two parts of the young nation, it was necessary to protect the coaches to insure that the stage made it through. Naturally, an agent like Hardie was needed to see that things ran smoothly and operated correctly and according to plan. Thus there would be the usual assortment of shootouts and other related problems, and it was around these that the series revolved.

Initially a half-hour series, it went to an hour in 1961 and moved from Mondays to Saturdays, but the stage was in the process of pulling into the final depot. Although he still worked for Wells Fargo and could occasionally be counted upon to take a special assignment, the extra half-hour gave Hardie time to hold down a ranch outside of San Francisco. As a result, most of the shows during the final season took place on the ranch. Apparently, however, the public didn't care for a domesticated Hardie, and he rode off into the sunset at the conclusion of that season.

Recorded Theme Music: "Tales of Wells Fargo," the Prairie Chiefs, RCA Children's Bluebird Records.

## The Tall Man
### NBC, September 1960–September 1962

Television, reflecting the wisdom of those who make the decisions and write the scripts, often has a way of making a sympathetic character out of someone you definitely wouldn't want your daughter to bring home. Although it hasn't as yet attempted to make a mass murderer seem like a poor, misunderstood slob who just happened to gun down 23 people on his way to church one Sunday, there have been attempts to glamorize the likes of the James Boys, Jesse and Frank. "The Tall Man" likewise presented William Bonney (aka Billy the Kid) in a sympathetic light, so that what we got were highly fictionalized stories about two real characters, set in New Mexico in the 1870s.

Billy (Clu Gulager) and Deputy Sheriff Pat Garrett (Barry Sullivan) were acquainted, and perhaps they might have had a few beers together in real life. However, what the series never showed was the climax of their lives, when Garrett wound up killing Billy. What it did show was a Pat Garrett, nicknamed "the Tall Man" because of his honesty and integrity, who looked upon Billy as a son or younger brother despite the fact they eventually would have to shoot it out.

While Billy, about 5 feet 5 inches tall in real life, tended to look upon his gun as a compensating factor for his shortness, Garrett, a good shot in his own right, regarded it as something to be used only in an emergency, which of course occurred with great regularity.

## Tate
### NBC, June 1960–September 1960

David McLean appeared as Tate, a Civil War soldier whose left arm had been severely damaged by an explosion during the war, which

Veteran character actor Jack Elam made his mark in the movies, usually playing the heavy, but in 1963–64 he was United States Marshal George Taggart
on "Temple Houston." He also starred in the situation comedy "The Texas
Wheelers" in 1974–75 and on "The Dakotas" in early 1963.

meant he was unable to find any kind of work once the war ended. As
a result, he became a wandering gunfighter in this series, which was
a summer replacement for the second half-hour of "The Perry Como
Show."

# Temple Houston
*NBC, September 1963–September 1964*

Another series based on a real-life character, Houston, as played by Jeffrey Hunter, was the attorney son of the legendary Sam Houston, the hero of the Texas War for Independence. During the 1880s, Houston, along with itinerant United States Marshal and former gunfighter George Taggart (Jack Elam), traveled the circuit court route, finding his clients wherever the court happened to be in session. In addition to possessing great oratorical skills which meant he usually won the case, Houston was also adept at using a gun (wasn't everyone?) and wouldn't hesitate to use it if necessary. Taggart, meanwhile, would hire himself out to the local town and, depending upon Houston's clients, would either be his friend or his nemesis.

# The Texan
*CBS, September 1958–September 1960*

Veteran actor Rory Calhoun was Bill Longley in what amounted to "The Restless Gun Moves to Texas." Following the Civil War, Longley became well known as a fast gun, good friend, and one who was out to insure that the law was obeyed even though he never wore a badge. After the series died, Calhoun chose to concentrate on movies and occasional guest shots on TV.

# Texas John Slaughter

As the title implies, John Slaughter was a Texan, and as the theme song of this Disney miniseries went, he "made 'em do what they oughta and if they didn't they'd die."

Tom Tryon starred as the peace officer determined to bring law and order to the Old West. (So what else was new?)

Unlike the other Disney actors, who remained in Hollywood (Parker and Loggia as actors and Courtland as a director), Tryon moved to the Northeast and became a best-selling author in the mid-1970s, penning such novels as *Harvest Home* and *The Other*.

# Tombstone Territory
*ABC, October 1957–October 1959*

Tombstone, Arizona, was known as the "the town too tough to die," and at one time or another, most of the Old West's famous gunmen and outlaws passed through. Naturally, a series had to be built around that fact, so Sheriff Clay Hollister (Pat Conway) was given the task of keeping law and order in that legendary Arizona community. Harris Claibourne (Richard Eastham) was the editor of *The Epitaph*, Tombstone's aptly named newspaper. Eastham, who was later to appear as General Blankenship on the comic-strip series "Wonder Woman," was also the host and narrator.

# Trackdown
*CBS, October 1957–September 1959*

Still another Texas Ranger keeping law and order, Robert Culp was Hoby Gilman, who during the 1870s attempted to keep things safe and secure for residents of the Lone Star State, tracking down outlaws and keeping peace between the Indians and the settlers. Many of the stories used in the series were adapted from actual cases in the Texas Rangers' files; the series had the official approval of the famous law enforcement agency and the state of Texas, a distinction not even the series "Tales of the Texas Rangers" could claim. Culp, who rode to and from the studio on a motorcycle, later starred in the superhero spoof "The Greatest American Hero" and in the spy series "I Spy" (with Bill Cosby).

# The Travels of Jamie McPheeters
*ABC, September 1963–March 1964*

Exactly what can you say that's good about a program which featured among its cast the singing Osmond Brothers (who, fortunately, never sang) as the Kissel Brothers, whose God-fearing parents gave them the names of Micah, Leviticus, Deuteronomy, and Lamentations? Probably the less said, the better, but they were there along with Kurt Russell as 12-year-old Jamie, whose father, Dr. Sardius McPheeters (Dan O'Herlihy), had sneaked out of Paducah, Kentucky, one step ahead of his creditors.

Linc Murdock (Charles Bronson) became wagonmaster shortly after the series began when the original wagonmaster, Buck Coulter (Michael Witney), died after saving Jamie's life. Also along for the ride to the gold mines of California in 1849 were the aristocratic Henry T. Coe (Hedley Mattingly) and his valet, Othello (Vernett Allen III), as well as 17-year-old orphan Jenny (Donna Anderson), Bible-quoting thief John Murrel (James Westerfield), and Murrel's accomplice, Shep Baggott (Sandy Kenyon).

## 26 Men
### Syndicated

By law, the Arizona Rangers were limited to 26 men, who were expected to maintain law and order in the entire territory around the turn of the century. Tris Coffin was featured as Captain Tom Rynning, and Kelso Henderson appeared as Ranger Clint Travis. Coffin, incidentally, had been one of the early television newsmen, hosting the current events program "Washington Report" on the DuMont network in 1951.

## Union Pacific
### Syndicated

Jeff Morrow, whose acting credits included *The Robe* and the romantic lead in *Captain Lightfoot*, took to the rails as Bart McClelland, the operations manager of the Union Pacific Railroad. A West Point graduate and former cavalry major, McClelland kept running into pesky Indians who were attempting to foil his goal of spanning California so there would be a link to Omaha, assuming anyone wanted to be linked to Omaha.

## The Virginian
### NBC, September 1962–September 1971

You never knew his name; he was simply known as "The Virginian" during the show's nine-year run, all of which was spent in a 90-minute period on Wednesday evenings (though the series was retitled "The Men from Shiloh" in its final season). But it didn't make that much difference what his name was, because you never knew the full names of most of the characters on the program, and it seemed that at times you would need a scorecard to keep track of the various characters that kept coming and going.

Along with the Virginian (James Drury) there was Trampas (Doug McClure), both of whom were the only characters to remain with the series the duration of its network run. Other one-name characters included Steve (Gary Clarke, 1962–64), Betsy (Roberta Shore, 1962–65), Randy (Randy Boone, 1963–66), Jennifer (Diane Roter, 1965–66), and Parker (John McLiam, 1970–71). In addition to the one-name characters, there were some who had both a first and last name, including Judge Henry Garth (Lee J. Cobb, 1962–66), Molly Wood (Pippa Scott, 1962–63), Emmett Ryker (Clu Gulager, 1964–68), John Grainger (Charles Bickford, 1966–67), Stacy Grainger (Don Quine, 1966–68), Elizabeth Grainger (Sara Lane, 1966–67), Clay Grainger (John McIntire, 1967–68), David Sutton (David Hartman, 1968–69), Jim Horn (Tim Matheson, 1969–70), Col. Alan MacKenzie (Stewart Granger, 1970–71), and Roy Tate (Lee Majors, 1970–71).

The first and most successful of the 90-minute Westerns, the show was set on the Shiloh Ranch somewhere in the Wyoming Territory near the turn of the century. During its nine years, the ranch was owned first by Judge Garth; later by the two Grainger brothers, John and Clay; and in its final year by Col. Alan MacKenzie. By the time MacKenzie had taken over the ranch, time had actually moved forward, which it seldom seemed to do in Westerns or any other series, and 1900 was just around the corner.

When the series made it to the air, it was substantially different from the pilot film shown on the dramatic anthology series "Decision" in the summer of 1958. Drury then appeared as an Eastern dandy.

The show was based on Owen Wister's 1902 novel of the same name, which had been made into a movie three times, the most famous no doubt being the 1929 version which starred Gary Cooper.

# Wagon Train
*NBC, September 1957–September 1962*
*ABC, September 1962–September 1965*

The wagons rolled westward from St. Joseph, Missouri, in 1957 on NBC and continued rolling there until 1962. They then rolled on over

**The late Ward Bond was Major Seth Adams in the original version of "Wagon Train." Following his death prior to the start of the 1961–62 season, the role of wagonmaster was turned over to John McIntire, who held the role until the wagons stopped rolling.**

to ABC, where the wagons kept on moving westward for three more years. In between, the lead character died and the series expanded to 90 minutes for one season. The program at times seemed more like a repertory company than one in which there were specific characters in continuing roles. Relying more on the strong characterizations of both the regular cast and guest stars and less on gimmicks — although it had a few — every episode was the story of someone, an excellent idea that seemed to work surprisingly well.

    Originally, the train was headed by Major Seth Adams, portrayed by Hollywood veteran Ward Bond, who provided a fatherly influence in the early going from 1957 to 1961. Bond, who had an engineering degree from the University of Southern California, appeared in over 150 feature films before his death prior to the start of the 1961–62 TV season. Following his death, the role of wagonmaster was given to John McIntire, who as Chris Hale served in the wagonmaster capacity until the train reached California for the last time.

Of the original cast, only Bill Hawks (Terry Wilson) and the cook, Charlie Wooster (Frank McGrath), were with the show throughout its eight-year trek across the plains, deserts, and mountains. Scout Flint McCullough (Robert Horton) left the series following the 1962 season vowing to never do another Western, only to turn up in "A Man Called Shenandoah" on ABC in 1965–66. Following Horton's departure, the scouting duties were taken over by Duke Shannon (Scott Miller) from 1961 to 1964 and Cooper Smith (Robert Fuller) from 1963 to 1965. The only other regular cast member was Barnaby West (Michael Burns), an orphaned 13-year-old the crew found along the way during the 1963 season.

By its second season, the show had moved into the Top 10 for the year, placing a close second to "Gunsmoke" for three consecutive years before moving into the top spot for the 1961–62 season.

Numerous stories centered around the conflicts of the series regulars, particularly prior to 1961, but just as many (if not more) were based on the conflicts, adventures, and misadventures of many top-name guest stars such as Burgess Meredith and a pair of Hollywood lovebirds named Ronald Reagan and Nancy Davis. In addition, there were the usual adventures featuring Indians, dry water holes, endless deserts, the Rockies, and even the occasional outlaw and his gang of desperadoes. Often the regular cast members found themselves either co-starring with, or in a role subservient to, the guest star, which gave the series more a feeling of a Western movie than a continuing series, especially after it had expanded to a 90-minute format.

As might be expected, the series was set in the 1870s following the Civil War, when westward expansion was at its peak.

In order to develop a feeling for the country before starting work on the series, Horton, who had served in the Coast Guard during World War II, got his feet on dry land by driving the entire route from St. Joseph's to California.

Recorded Theme Music: "Wagon Train," Sons of the Pioneers, RCA Children's Bluebird Records.

# Wanted: Dead or Alive
*CBS, September 1958–March 1961*

This series made Steve McQueen a star, that much is certain. Did it make any difference that he had played a teenager in the less-than-memorable horror movie *The Blob* just a short time before? When he strapped on his gun, a sawed-off carbine he called his "mare's leg," he became Josh Randall, bounty hunter, a man of few words who was long on action. It was the series that first brought him to the attention of the general public.

Although he was a bounty hunter, Randall, unlike most of that ilk, was haunted by his conscience and as a result would try to capture a man instead of shooting him. Weekly, Randall would wander from town to town, picking up his assignment from the "Wanted" posters, and would usually run into either another bounty hunter or a lawman who had no respect for bounty hunters. In addition to the obligatory showdown with the desperado, there always seemed to be a number of reasons for nonstop action, and the series delivered it faithfully.

# Western Marshal
*Syndicated*

The title says it all. Douglas Kennedy was a marshal out West and each week could be counted upon to bring the bad guys to justice.

# The Westerner
*NBC, September 1960–December 1960*

Before he became domesticated, with a butler no less, on the long-running situation comedy "Family Affair," Brian Keith was Dave Blassingame, a wanderer who, accompanied by his dog, Brown, fought the bad guys for several months. He eventually wanted to settle down and breed quarter horses but instead had to settle for Buffy and Jody—not to mention Mr. French—six years later. After "Family Affair" went to the Nielsen heaven, it was to be some time before Keith tried another series, and it was to be the long-running adventure series "Hardcastle and McCormick."

Douglas Kennedy starred as the Western Marshal in the syndicated series of the same name. Basically a run-of-the-mill Western, it wasn't around very long and marked Kennedy's sole television attempt at a starring role.

# Westward Ho! The Wagons

Actually, this was a movie, but as was frequently the case with Disney, after it had completed its run in the theaters it popped up on TV, running for several weeks as a miniseries (before anyone else had ever thought of the concept) under the "Frontierland" banner. Fess Parker made his return to the Disney studios as John Grayson, but failed to repeat his Davy Crockett success. As the name implies, it was all about this wagon train headed West....

Recorded Theme Music: "Westward Ho! The Wagons," Fess Parker, Columbia Records. "Westward Ho! The Wagons," Bill Hayes,

Columbia Records. "Westward Ho! The Wagons," Vaughn Monroe, RCA Children's Bluebird Records.

# Whispering Smith
### NBC, May 1961–September 1961

Somewhat of a forerunner to, although not nearly as successful as, Richard Boone's "Hec Ramsey," this show gave the late Audie Murphy a chance to try TV. He portrayed Denver police detective Tom Smith ("Just call me 'Whispering,' everyone does"), who relied upon the latest methods of analysis and detection in solving crimes. He was aided—but not for long—by his partner and sidekick, George Romack (Guy Mitchell).

Murphy, one of the most decorated war heroes of World War II, had appeared in numerous movie Westerns, the most successful perhaps, being *Destry*. A better singer than actor, Mitchell topped the country and pop charts in the mid-1950s with the song "Singin' the Blues." Several more of his records also made the charts, and he hosted his own musical variety series on ABC in 1957–58.

# Wichita Town
### NBC, September 1959–September 1960

Veteran Western movie and radio actor Joel McRae took a fling at a weekly television series in 1959, along with his son, Jody, in this tale based upon the attempts to bring law and order to Wichita, Kansas (in the Kansas territory naturally), in the decade following the Civil War.

As Mike Dunbar, the elder McRae portrayed the town's leading citizen, a man who had stayed on as marshal following the conclusion of a cattle drive. He was aided by two deputies, Ben Matheson (son Jody) and Rico Rodriguez (Carlos Romero), a former Mexican gunfighter who was now foreman at the nearby Circle J Ranch.

# The Wide Country
### NBC, September 1962–September 1963

Earl Holliman was Mitch Guthrie, a champion bronc rider, and Andrew Prine was his brother, Andy. Stories centered around the

Bearing about as much resemblance to the real Wild Bill Hickok as Hugh
O'Brian did to the real Wyatt Earp, Guy Madison (*left*) portrayed the fabled
marshal for a number of years in a syndicated series that was immensely
popular with the younger set. His partner, Jingles Jones (*right*), was portrayed
by veteran character actor Andy Devine.

adventures encountered with the rodeo while Mitch tried to persuade
his brother to find an honest line of work.

# Wild Bill Hickok
*Syndicated*

Guy Madison, who had appeared in more "B" films than just about anybody, resembled the real Marshal James Butler Hickok in name only. Where the real Hickok was a scruffy type who wore a long black coat and achieved about as much notoriety as a gambler as he did as marshal, the TV version featured a squeaky-clean Hickok complete with a fringed buckskin jacket. His sidekick was Jingles Jones (Andy Devine), who, it seemed, was always crying out, "Hey Wild Bill, wait for me."

Aimed strictly at the younger audience, it first popped up briefly on CBS on Saturday afternoons, then quickly moved on into syndication, where it remained a staple for a number of years.

Like many others, it had a companion series on the radio, the radio version hitting the air on December 31, 1951. Both Madison and Devine portrayed the same roles in what was basically the same series that went to the small screen.

# The Wild Wild West
*CBS, September 1965–September 1970*

Actually, new episodes of "The Wild Wild West" ran for only a little over four years, with the last three months being reruns of earlier episodes airing as a summer replacement. The show revolved around undercover agent James T. West (Robert Conrad) and sidekick Artemus Gordon (Ross Martin), who proved that the West really was wild. Or maybe it was James T. West who was wild; it really made no difference.

The James Bond movies were in vogue when the series was launched, and with the public's appetite whetted for superheroes, gimmicks, beautiful women, and unbelievable situations, the series took off. Although never an outstanding ratings smash, winding up in the Top 25 only once, the series quickly developed a cult following much like that garnered by "Star Trek" and "The Man from U.N.C.L.E." (meaning that there are devotees who even today can recite every plot, every gimmick, and even the dialogue).

Basically, the series concerned the adventures of West and Gordon, the latter a master of disguises and dialects, who were undercover agents for President U.S. Grant. Together, they attempted to undo the efforts of radical and subversive groups as well as criminal elements that were attempting to set up their own little kingdoms using all or part of the United States or any other number of possibilities. If Bond and the men from U.N.C.L.E. had strange weapons that could accomplish anything imaginable, so did West and Gordon — particularly considering the time in which they operated.

Although it's highly unlikely anyone took the episodes seriously, they definitely provided a welcome respite from the turmoil of the late 1960s.

Prior to becoming James West, Conrad had starred in "Hawaiian Eye" on ABC from 1959 to 1963 and attempted to use his popularity in that series as a springboard to a singing career in the early 1960s. Although the records weren't major hits, they are sought after today by record collectors and, when found, bring premium prices.

Proving there was life after James T. West, Conrad moved to the courtroom in 1971–72, starring in "The D.A." on NBC. When it failed, he starred the following season in a spy series, "Assignment Vienna" on ABC, but it wasn't until he starred in the World War II drama "Baa Baa Black Sheep" from 1976 to 1978 on NBC that he had another hit series.

# Wrangler
## NBC, August 1960–September 1960

As the summer replacement for Tennessee Ernie Ford, this series wasn't expected to have a long life, and it didn't. Jason Evers, a veteran actor who should have known better, was Pitcairn the Wrangler. Sometimes a ranch hand and sometimes a gunfighter, he could be counted upon to get into at least one fight per week, with the expected allotment of blood being spilled.

# Yancy Derringer
## CBS, October 1958–September 1959

Three years after the Civil War had ended, New Orleans was a target for carpetbaggers, smugglers, and just about every type of scoundrel you could name or think of. Since the South was still resentful toward the federal government, a method to help the people had to be found. Into this scenario entered Yancy Derringer (Jock Mahoney), an ex–Confederate soldier turned card sharp and adventurer who was actually a special agent working for John Colton (Kevin Hagen), the civil administrator of the city of New Orleans.

Derringer's right-hand man was the Pawnee Indian Pahoo-Ka Ta Wah (X. Brands), referred to by Derringer as a "fine, clean-cut savage," whose cleverness frequently got Derringer out of numerous scrapes. Under his blanket, Pahoo carried a sawed-off shotgun, with a knife or small pistol hidden under his hair, depending upon the occasion.

Although far apart in background and upbringing, the pair could be counted upon to prevent crimes when it was possible and to catch the criminals when it was not. A fancy dresser, suave and sophisticated, Derringer toted only one weapon: a tiny single-shot derringer, which he carried in his hat.

Mahoney, a Hollywood veteran, had started his career as a stunt man, taking the falls for such stars as Gregory Peck, Randolph Scott, and Errol Flynn, whom he resembled. His only other starring role in a series was in the syndicated "Range Rider," for which he shaved off his mustache.

# Young Dan'l Boone
*CBS, September 1977–October 1977*

To this less-than-spectacular series goes the honor of being axed faster, with fewer episodes being produced, than any other Western or frontier drama in the history of television. Someone had to have that dubious honor, and it might as well have been this series, which was certainly deserving.

Not much was accomplished in the four weeks young Daniel, or Dan'l if you prefer (Rick Moses), explored the Kentucky hills and woods with his companions, Peter Dawes (John Joseph Thomas), a 12-year-old English boy, Hawk (Ji-Tu Cumbuka), a runaway slave, and a Cherokee Indian named Tsiskwa (Eloy Phil Casados) (whatever happened to Mingo?) while his sweetheart, Rebecca Ryan (Devon Ericson), waited for him at home. She obviously didn't have to wait long. Fess Parker as an older Daniel did it much better.

# Zorro
## *ABC, October 1957–September 1959*

Throughout the long history of television, only one series has ever started with the letter "Z." Like Davy Crockett, which came from the same studio, Zorro spawned a whole mini-industry, thanks in large part (no doubt) to the fact that Walt Disney was the studio. There were Zorro bubblegum cards, lunchboxes, notebooks, anything that could make a buck. A complete mint set of Zorro bubblegum cards (88 cards) is worth about $75 today. The wrapper alone is worth about $30. And, while Zorro was somewhat tame in comparison to the other heroes on the tube, the kids seemed to love him.

The legend of the masked Zorro, running around California in the 1820s, has given rise to numerous movies, Saturday morning theatrical serials, comic books, novels, and just about everything else imaginable. Even though the character never existed, Zorro proved to be a Hollywood favorite and will no doubt someday return, probably placed in Texas or Arizona. For those who follow the legend, the television version has proved to be the most popular, and perhaps most enduring; when people mention Zorro in their nostalgic reminiscences, this is probably the Zorro they have in mind, not the Clayton Moore version.

Guy Williams, who was to later star in the kiddie science-fiction series "Lost in Space" from 1965 to 1968, was Zorro (given name: Don Diego de la Vega), the mysterious masked and caped avenger who, in 1820, returned to California at the urging of his father, Don Alejandro (George J. Lewis). Arriving in California, Don Diego appeared to be very much the aristocratic gentleman, one who in no way would dare oppose the evil Captain Monastario (Britt Lomond), the ruthless army officer who had become commandant of the Fortress de Los Angeles and who was terrorizing the locals.

Unknown to anyone other than his faithful deaf-mute servant Bernardo (Gene Sheldon), Diego periodically donned Zorro's mask, cape, and sword and set out on one of his two horses, the black Toronado and the white Phantom, depending upon the occasion, to right the wrongs perpetrated by Monastario. Why no one ever figured out that the appearance of Zorro occurred at just about the same time Don Diego returned home is a mystery, but Monastario had his suspicions.

With a number of sword fights, the show rapidly became a

children's favorite, aided no doubt by the fact that both Monastario and his fat, dimwitted aide, Sgt. Garcia (Henry Calvin), always wound up getting their just desserts in the end.

Also appearing in the series on a regular basis were Jan Arvan as Nacho Torres, Vinton Hayworth as Magistrate Galindo, Jolene Brand as Anna Maria Verdugo (Don Diego's love interest in the second season), Eduard Franz as her father, Senor Gregario Verdugo, and Don Diamond as Corporal Reyes.

Recorded Theme Music: "Zorro," The Chordettes, Cadence Records. This was the hit version. However, the version heard on television was done by none other than Henry Calvin (yes, Sgt. Garcia). Released on the Disney-owned Buena Vista Records, it is considered quite rare.

# Appendix A
## The Actors and Their Roles

**The Adventures of Davy Crockett**
Fess Parker *Davy Crockett*
Buddy Ebsen *Georgie Russell*

**The Adventures of Jim Bowie**
Scott Forbes *Jim Bowie*
Robert Cornthwaite *John James Audubon*
Peter Hanson *Rezin Bowie*

**The Adventures of Kit Carson**
Bill Williams *Kit Carson*
Don Diamond *El Toro*

**The Adventures of Rin Tin Tin**
Lee Aaker *Rusty*
James Brown *Lt. Rip Masters*
Joe Sawyer *Sgt. Biff O'Hara*
Rand Brooks *Cpl. Boone*

**The Alaskans**
Roger Moore *Silky Harris*
Jeff York *Reno McKee*
Ray Danton *Nifty Cronin*
Dorothy Provine *Rocky Shaw*

**Alias Smith and Jones**
Ben Murphy *Jed "Kid" Curry*

Pete Duel *Hannibal Heyes (1971)*
Roger Davis *Hannibal Heyes (1972-1973)*
Sally Field *Clementine Hale*

**The Americans**
Darryl Hickman *Ben Canfield*
Dick Davalos *Jeff Canfield*

**Annie Oakley**
Gail Davis *Annie Oakley*
Brad Johnson *Lofty Craig*
Jimmy Hoskins *Tag Oakley*

**The Barbary Coast**
William Shatner *Jeff Cable*
Doug McClure *Cash Conover*
Richard Kiel *Moose Moran*

**Bat Masterson**
Gene Barry *Bat Masterson*

**The Big Valley**
Barbara Stanwyck *Victoria Barkley*
Lee Majors *Heath Barkley*
Linda Evans *Audra Barkley*
Richard Long *Jarrod Barkley*
Peter Breck *Nick Barkley*
Napolean Whiting *Silas, the Butler*

**Black Saddle**
Peter Breck *Clay Culhane*
Russell Johnson *Marshal Gib Scott*

**Bonanza**
Lorne Greene *Ben Cartwright*
Pernell Roberts *Adam Cartwright*
Michael Landon *Little Joe
  Cartwright*
Dan Blocker *Hoss Cartwright*
Victor Sen Yung *Hop Sing*
David Canary *Candy*
Lou Frizzell *Dusty Rhoades*
Mitch Vogel *Jamie Hunter*
Tim Matheson *Griff King*

**Boots and Saddles**
Jack Pickard *Shank Adams*
Michael Hinn *Luke Cummings*

**Branded**
Chuck Connors *Jason McCord*

**Brave Eagle**
Keith Larsen *Brave Eagle*
Keena Nomkeena *Keena*
Kim Winona *Morning Star*
Bert Wheeler *Smokey Joe*

**Broken Arrow**
John Lupton *Tom Jeffords*
Michael Ansara *Cochise*

**Bronco**
Ty Hardin *Bronco Layne*

**Buckskin**
Tommy Nolan *Jody O'Connell*
Sallie Brophy *Annie O'Connell*
Michael Road *Tom Sellers*

**Buffalo Bill, Jr.**
Dick Jones *Buffalo Bill, Jr.*

**The Californians**
Richard Coogan *Matthew Wayne*
Adam Kennedy *Dion Patrick*
Herbert Rudley *Sam Brennan*
Sean McClory *Jack McGivern*
Carole Mathews *Wilma Fansler*
Arthur Fleming *Jeremy Pitt*

**Cheyenne**
Clint Walker *Cheyenne Bodie*
L.Q. Jones *Smitty*

**Cimarron City**
George Montgomery *Matthew
  Rockford*
Dan Blocker *Tiny Budinger*
Audrey Totter *Beth Purcell*
John Smith *Lane Temple*
Stuart Randall *Art Sampson*
Addison Richards *Martin Kingsley*
Fred Sherman *Burt Purdy*
Claire Carleton *Alice Purdy*
George Dunn *Jesse Williams*
Pete Dunn *Dody Hammer*
Tom Fadden *Silas Perry*
Wally Brown *Jed Fame*

**Cimarron Strip**
Stuart Whitman *Jim Crown*
Randy Boone *Francis Wilde*
Percy Herbert *Mac Gregor*
Jill Townsend *Dulcy Coopersmith*

**The Cisco Kid**
Duncan Renaldo *Cisco*
Leo Carillo *Pancho*

**Colt .45**
Wayde Preston *Christopher Colt*
Donald May *Sam Colt, Jr.*

**Cowboy in Africa**
Chuck Connors *Jim Sinclair*

Ronald Howard *Howard Hayes*
Tom Nardini *John Henry*
Gerald Edwards *Sampson*

**Cowboy Theatre**
Monty Hall *Host*

**The Cowboys**
Moses Gunn *Jebediah Nightlinger*
Diana Douglas *Annie Anderson*
Jim Davis *Bill Winter*
A. Martinez *Cimarron*
Robert Carradine *Slim*
Sean Kelly *Jimmy*
Kerry MacLane *Homer*
Clint Howard *Steve*
Mitch Brown *Hardy*
Clay O'Brien *Weedy*

**Custer**
Wayne Maunder *George Armstrong Custer*
Slim Pickens *Joe Milner*
Grant Woods *Capt. Miles Keogh*
Peter Palmer *Sgt. James Bustard*
Michael Dante *Crazy Horse*
Robert F. Simon *Brig. Gen. Alfred Terry*

**The Dakotas**
Larry Ward *Frank Ragan*
Jack Elam *J.D. Smith*
Chad Everett *Del Stark*
Mike Greene *Vance Porter*

**Daniel Boone**
Fess Parker *Daniel Boone*
Patricia Blair *Rebecca Boone*
Ed Ames *Mingo*
Darby Hinton *Israel Boone*
Veronica Cartwright *Jemima Boone*
Dal McKennon *Cincinnatus*

Robert Logan *Jericho Jones*
Don Pedro Colley *Gideon*
Roosevelt Grier *Gabe Cooper*
Jimmy Dean *Josh Clements*
Albert Salmi *Yadkin*

**Death Valley Days**
Stanley Adams *Host (The Old Ranger)*
Ronald Reagan *Host*

**The Deputy**
Henry Fonda *Simon Fry*
Allen Case *Clay McCord*
Wallace Ford *Herk Lamson*
Betty Lou Keim *Fran McCord*
Read Morgan *Hap Tasker*

**Destry**
John Gavin *Harrison Destry*

**Dick Powell's Zane Grey Theatre**
Dick Powell *Host*

**Dirty Sally**
Jeanette Nolan *Sally Fergus*
Dack Rambo *Cyrus Pike*

**Dundee and the Culhane**
John Mills *Dundee*
Sean Garrison *The Culhane*

**Empire**
Richard Egan *Jim Redigo*
Terry Moore *Constance Garrett*
Anne Seymour *Lucia Garrett*
Ryan O'Neal *Tal Garrett*
Warren Vanders *Chuck*
Charles Bronson *Paul Moreno*

**Frontier**
Walter Coy *Host*

**Frontier Circus**
Chill Wills *Col. Casey Thompson*
John Derek *Ben Travis*
Richard Jaeckel *Tony Gentry*

**Frontier Justice**
Lew Ayres *Host (1958)*
Melvyn Douglas *Host (1959)*
Ralph Bellamy *Host (1961)*

**Gabby Hayes**
Gabby Hayes *Host*

**The Gene Autry Show**
Gene Autry and Pat Buttram *as themselves*

**The Gray Ghost**
Tod Andrews *John Singleton Mosby*

**The Guns of Will Sonnett**
Walter Brennan *Will Sonnett*
Dack Rambo *Jeff Sonnett*
Jason Evers *James Sonnett*

**Gunslinger**
Tony Young *Cord*
Preston Foster *Capt. Zachary Wingate*
Charles Gray *Pico McGuire*
Dee Pollock *Billy Urchin*

**Gunsmoke**
James Arness *Matt Dillon*
Milburn Stone *Doc Adams*
Amanda Blake *Kitty Russell*
Ken Curtis *Festus Haggen*
Dennis Weaver *Chester Goode*
Glenn Strange *Sam, the bartender*
Buck Taylor *Newly O'Brien*
Burt Reynolds *Quint Asper*
Roger Ewing *Thad Greenwood*

**Have Gun, Will Travel**
Richard Boone *Paladin*
Kam Tong *Hey Boy*
Lisa Lu *Hey Girl*

**Heck Ramsey**
Richard Boone *Hec Ramsey*
Richard Lenz *Oliver B. Stamp*
Harry Morgan *Dr. Amos Coogan*
Dennis Rucker *Arne Tornquist*

**The High Chaparral**
Leif Erickson *John Cannon*
Cameron Mitchell *Buck Cannon*
Henry Darrow *Manolito Montoya*
Linda Cristal *Victoria Cannon*
Mark Slade *Billy Blue Cannon*
Don Collier *Sam Butler*
Robert Hoy *Joe*
Frank Silvera *Don Sebastian Montoya*
Roberto Contreras *Pedro*
Ted Markland *Reno*
Rudy Ramos *Wind*

**Hondo**
Ralph Taeger *Hondo Lane*
Gary Clarke *Capt. Richards*
Noah Beery, Jr. *Buffalo Baker*
Kathie Browne *Angie Dow*
Buddy Foster *Johnny Dow*

**Hopalong Cassidy**
William Boyd *Hopalong Cassidy*
Edgar Buchanan *Red Connors*

**Hotel de Paree**
Earl Holliman *Sundance*
Jeanette Nolan *Annette Deveraux*
Judi Meredith *Monique*

**How the West Was Won**
James Arness *Zeb Macahan*

Bruce Boxleitner *Luke Macahan*
Kathryn Holcomb  *Laura Macahan*
Vicki Schreck *Jessie Macahan*
William Kirby Cullen *Josh
  Macahan*
Fionnula Flanagan *Molly Culhane*

**The Iron Horse**
Dale Robertson *Ben Calhoun*
Garry Collins *Dave Tarrant*
Roger Torrey *Nils*
Bob Random *Barnabas Rogers*
Ellen McRae *Julie Parsons*

**Jefferson Drum**
Jeff Richards *Jefferson Drum*
Eugene Martin *Joey Drum*
Cyril Delavanti *Lucius Cain*
Robert Stevenson *Big Ed*

**Johnny Ringo**
Don Durant *Johnny Ringo*
Mark Goddard *Cully*
Karen Sharpe *Laura Thomas*
Terence de Marney *Case Thomas*

**Judge Roy Bean**
Edgar Buchanan *Judge Roy Bean*

**Klondike**
Ralph Taeger *Mike Halliday*
James Coburn *Jeff Durain*
Mari Blanchard *Kathy O'Hara*
Joi Lansing *Goldie*

**Kung Fu**
David Carradine *Caine*
Radames Pera *Young Caine*
Keye Luke *Master Po*
Philip Ahn *Master Kan*
Season Hubley *Margit*

**Lancer**
Andrew Duggan *Murdoch Lancer*
Wayne Maunder *Scott Lancer*
James Stacy *Johnny Lancer*
Elizabeth Baur *Teresa O'Brien*
Paul Brinegar *Jelly Hoskins*

**Laramie**
John Smith *Slim Sherman*
Robert Fuller *Jess Harper*
Bobby Crawford, Jr. *Andy Harper*
Hoagy Carmichael *Jonesy*
Stuart Randall *Mort Corey*
Dennis Holmes *Mike Williams*
Spring Byington *Daisy Cooper*

**Laredo**
Neville Brand *Reese Bennett*
William Smith *Joe Riley*
Peter Brown *Chad Cooper*
Philip Carey *Captain Parmalee*
Robert Wolders *Erik Hunter*

**Law of the Plainsman**
Michael Ansara *Sam Buckhart*
Dayton Lummi *Andy Morrison*
Gina Gillespie *Tess Logan*
Nora Marlowe *Martha Commager*

**The Lawman**
John Russell *Dan Troop*
Peter Brown *Johnny McKay*
Peggy Castle *Lily Merrill*
Dan Sheridan *Jake*

**The Legend of Jesse James**
Christopher Jones *Jesse James*
Allen Case *Frank James*
John Milford *Cole Younger*
Tim McIntire *Bob Younger*
Robert Wilke *Sam Corbett*

**The Life and Legend of Wyatt Earp**
Hugh O'Brian *Wyatt Earp*
Douglas Fowley *Doc Holliday*
Myron Healy *Doc Holliday*
Mason Alan Dinehart *Bat Masterson*
Denver Pyle *Ben Thompson*
Hal Baylor *Bill Thompson*
Gloria Talbot *Abbie Crandall*
Don Haggerty *Marsh Murdock*
Douglas Fowley *Doc Fabrique*
Paul Brinegar *Jim "Dog" Kelly*
Ralph Sanford *Jim "Dog" Kelly*
Selmer Jackson *Mayor Hoover*
William Tanner *Hal Norton*
Morgan Woodward *Shotgun Gibbs*
Dirk London *Morgan Earp*
John Anderson *Virgil Earp*
Randy Stuart *Nellie Cashman*
Trevor Bardette *Ike Clanton*
Carol Thurston *Emma Clanton*
Lash LaRue *Sheriff Johnny Behan*
Steve Brodie *Sheriff Johnny Behan*
William Phipps *Curley Bill Brocius*
Britt Lomond *Johnny Ringo*
Stacy Harris *Mayor Clum*
Damian O'Flynn *Doc Goodfellow*
Lloyd Corrigan *Ned Buntline*

**The Life and Times of Grizzly Adams**
Dan Haggerty *Grizzly Adams*
Denver Pyle *Mad Jack*
Don Shanks *Nakuma*
John Bishop *Robbie Cartman*

**The Lone Ranger**
Clayton Moore *The Lone Ranger*
John Hart *The Lone Ranger (1952–54)*
Jay Silverheels *Tonto*

**The Loner**
Lloyd Bridges *William Colton*

**A Man Called Shenandoah**
Robert Horton *Shenandoah*

**The Man from Blackhawk**
Robert Rockwell *Sam Logan*

**The Marshal of Gunsight Pass**
Russell "Lucky" Hayden *The Marshal*
Roscoe Ates *His sidekick*

**Maverick**
James Garner *Bret Maverick*
Jack Kelly *Bart Maverick*
Roger Moore *Beauregard Maverick*
Robert Colbert *Brent Maverick*

**The Men from Shiloh**
See "The Virginian"

**The Monroes**
Liam Sullivan *Major Mapoy*
Ron Soble *Dirty Jim*
Michael Anderson, Jr. *Clayt Monroe*
Barbara Hershey *Kathy Monroe*
Keith Schultz *Jefferson Monroe*
Kevin Schultz *Fennimore Monroe*
Jim Westmoreland *Ruel Jaxon*
Ben Johnson *Sleeve*
Robert Middleton *Barney Wales*

**The New Land**
Bonnie Bedelia *Anna Larsen*
Scott Thomas *Christian Larsen*
Todd Lookinland *Tuliff Larsen*
Debbie Lytton *Annaliese Larsen*
Kurt Russell *Bo*

**The Nine Lives of Elfego Baca**
Robert Loggia *Elfego Baca*

**Nichols**
James Garner *Nichols/Jim Nichols*
Neva Patterson *Ma Ketcham*
Stuart Margolin *Mitch Ketcham*
Margot Kidder *Ruth*
Alice Ghostley *Bertha*

**Northwest Passage**
Buddy Ebsen *Sgt. Hunk Marriner*
Keith Larsen *Major Robert Rogers*
Don Burnett *Ensign Langdon
   Towne*

**The Oregon Trail**
Rod Taylor *Evan Thorpe*
Andrew Stevens *Andy Thorpe*
Tony Becker *William Thorpe*
Gina Marie Smika *Rachel Thorpe*
Darleen Carr *Margaret Devlin*
Charles Napier *Luther Sprague*

**The Outcasts**
Don Murray *Earl Corey*
Otis Young *Jemal David*

**The Outlaws**
Barton MacLane *Frank Caine*
Don Collier *Will Forman*
Jock Gaynor *Heck Martin*
Bruce Yarnell *Chalk Breeson*
Judy Lewis *Connie Masters*
Slim Pickens *Slim*

**The Overland Trail**
William Bendix *Frederick Thomas
   Kelly*
Doug McClure *Frank Flippen*

**The Quest**
Kurt Russell *Morgan Beaudine*
Tim Matheson *Quentin Beaudine*

**The Range Rider**
Jock Mahoney *The Range Rider*
Dick Jones *Dick West*

**Rawhide**
Eric Fleming *Gil Favor*
Clint Eastwood *Rowdy Yates*
Paul Brinegar *Wishbone*
Jim Quince *Steve Raines*
Sheb Wooley *Pete Nolan*
Rocky Shahan *Joe Scarlett*
James Murdock *Mushy*
Robert Cabal *Jesus Patines*
Charles Gray *Clay Forrester*
David Watson *Ian Cabot*
Raymond St. Jacques *Solomon
   King*

**The Rebel**
Nick Adams *Johnny Yuma*

**Redigo**
Richard Egan *Jim Redigo*
Roger Davis *Mike*
Rudy Solari *Frank Martinez*
Elena Verdugo *Gerry*

**The Restless Gun**
John Payne *Vint Bonner*

**The Rifleman**
Chuck Connors *Lucas McCain*
Johnny Crawford *Mark McCain*
Paul Fix *Micah Torrance*
Joan Taylor *Molly Scott*
Patricia Blair *Lou Mallory*

**Riverboat**
Darren McGavin *Grey Holden*
Burt Reynolds *Ben Frazer*
William D. Gordon *Travis*
Noah Beery *Bill Blake*

**The Road West**
Barry Sullivan *Benjamin Pride*
Kathryn Hays *Elizabeth Reynolds
  Pride*
Glenn Corbett *Chance Reynolds*
Andrew Prine *Timothy Pride*
Brenda Scott *Midge Pride*
Kelly Corcoran *Kip Pride*
Charles Seel *Grandpa Pride*

**The Rough Riders**
Kent Taylor *Jim Flagg*
Peter Whitney *Buck Sinclair*
Jan Merlin *Lt. Kirby*

**The Roy Rogers Show**
Roy Rogers, Dale Evans, and Pat
  Brady *as themselves.*

**The Saga of Andy Burnette**
Jerome Courtland *Andy Burnette*

**Sara**
Brenda Vaccaro *Sara Yarnell*
Bert Kramer *Emmett Ferguson*
William Phipps *Claude Barstow*
William Wintersole *George Bailey*
Albert Stratton *Martin Pope*
Mariclare Costello *Julia Bailey*
Louise Latham *Martha Higgins*

**Saturday Roundup**
Kermit Maynard *Host*

**Sergeant Preston of the Yukon**
Richard Simmons *Sergeant Preston*

**Shane**
David Carradine *Shane*
Jill Ireland *Marian Starett*
Tom Tully *Tom Starett*
Christopher Shea *Joey Starett*
Bert Freed *Rufe Ryker*
Sam Gilman *Sam Grafton*

**The Sheriff of Cochise**
John Bromfield *Sheriff*

**Shotgun Slade**
Scott Brady *Shotgun Slade*

**Sky King**
Kirby Grant *Sky King*
Gloria Winters *Penny*
Ron Haggerty *Clipper*

**Stagecoach West**
Wayne Rogers *Luke Perry*
Robert Bray *Simon Kane*
Richard Eyer *David Kane*

**The Swamp Fox**
Leslie Nielson *Francis Marion*

**Sugarfoot**
Will Hutchins *Tom Brewster*

**Tales of the Texas Rangers**
Willard Parker *Jace Pearson*
Harry Lauter *Clay Morgan*

**Tales of the West**
Jim Davis

**Tales of Wells Fargo**
Dale Robertson *Jim Hardie*

**The Tall Man**
Clu Gulager *Billy the Kid*
Barry Sullivan *Pat Garrett*

**Tate**
David McLean *Tate*

**Temple Houston**
Jeffrey Hunter *Temple Houston*
Jack Elam *George Taggart*

**The Texan**
Rory Calhoun *Bill Longley*

**Texas John Slaughter**
Tom Tryon *Texas John Slaughter*

**Tombstone Territory**
Pat Conway *Clay Hollister*
Richard Eastham *Harris Claibourne*

**Trackdown**
Robert Culp *Hoby Gilman*

**The Travels of Jamie McPheeters**
Kurt Russell *Jamie McPheeters*
Osmond Brothers *Kissel Brothers*
Dan O'Herlihy *Dr. Sardius McPheeters*
Charles Bronson *Linc Murdock*
Michael Witney *Buck Coulter*
Hedley Mattingly *Henry T. Coe*
Vernett Allen III *Othello*
Donna Anderson *Jenny*
James Westerfield *John Murrel*
Sandy Kenyon *Shep Baggott*

**26 Men**
Tris Coffin *Capt. Tom Rynning*
Kelso Henderson *Clint Travis*

**Union Pacific**
Jeff Morrow *Bart McClelland*

**The Virginian**
James Drury *The Virginian*
Doug McClure *Trampas*
Gary Clarke *Steve*
Roberta Shore *Betsy*
Randy Boone *Randy*
Diane Roter *Jennifer*
John McLiam *Parker*
Lee J. Cobb *Judge Henry Garth*

Pippa Scott *Molly Wood*
Clu Gulager *Emmett Ryker*
Charles Bickford *John Grainger*
Don Quine *Stacy Grainger*
Sara Lane *Elizabeth Grainger*
John McIntire *Clay Grainger*
Jeanette Nolan *Holly Grainger*
David Hartman *David Sutton*
Tim Matheson *Jim Horn*
Stewart Granger *Col. Alan MacKenzie*
Lee Majors *Roy Tate*

**Wagon Train**
Ward Bond *Major Seth Adams*
John McIntire *Chris Hale*
Terry Wilson *Bill Hawks*
Frank McGrath *Charlie Wooster*
Robert Horton *Flint McCullough*
Scott Miller *Duke Shannon*
Robert Fuller *Cooper Smith*
Michael Burns *Barnaby West*

**Wanted: Dead or Alive**
Steve McQueen *Josh Randall*

**The Western Marshal**
Douglas Kennedy

**The Westerner**
Brian Keith *Dave Blassingame*

**Westward Ho! The Wagons**
Fess Parker *John Grayson*

**Whispering Smith**
Audie Murphy *Tom "Whispering" Smith*
Guy Mitchell *George Romack*

**Wichita Town**
Joel McRae *Mike Dunbar*

Jody McRae *Ben Matheson*
Carlos Romero *Rico Rodriguez*

**Wild Bill Hickok**
Guy Madison *Wild Bill Hickok*
Andy Devine *Jingles Jones*

**The Wild Wild West**
Robert Conrad *James T. West*
Ross Martin *Artemus Gordon*

**Wrangler**
Jason Evers *Pitcairn, the Wrangler*

**Yancy Derringer**
Jock Mahoney *Yancy Derringer*
X. Brands *Pahoo-Ka Ta Wah*
Kevin Hagen *John Colton*

**Young Dan'l Boone**
Rick Moses *Daniel Boone*
John Joseph Thomas *Peter Dawes*
Ji-Tu Cumbuka *Hawk*
Eloy Phil Casados *Tsiskwa*
Devon Ericson *Rebecca Ryan*

**Zorro**
Guy Williams *Don Diego de la Vega (Zorro)*
Gene Sheldon *Bernardo*
Henry Calvin *Sgt. Garcia*
Britt Lomond *Captain Monastario*
George J. Lewis *Don Alejandro*
Jan Arvan *Nacho Torres*
Vinton Hayworth *Magistrate Galindo*
Jolene Brand *Anna Maria Verdugo*
Eduard Franz *Senor Gregorio Verdugo*
Don Diamond *Corporal Reyes*

# Appendix B
# Emmy Award Winners

Despite the disdain with which the Hollywood establishment looked upon Westerns, they were hard to ignore. In fact, over a twenty-year span, four different series won a total of five different awards.

**1958**
Best Dramatic Series with Continuing Characters:
"Gunsmoke"

**1959**
Best Supporting Actor (Continuing Character)
in a Dramatic Series:
Dennis Weaver
(Chester)
"Gunsmoke"

**1966**
Outstanding Continuing Performance by an
Actress in a Leading Role
in a Dramatic Series:
Barbara Stanwyck
(Victoria Barkley)
"The Big Valley"

**1973**
Outstanding Directorial Achievement
in Series Drama
Jerry Thorpe
"An Eye for an Eye" —
Episode of "Kung Fu"

**1978**
Outstanding Single Performance by a Supporting Actor
in a Comedy or Drama Series:
Ricardo Montalban
"How the West Was Won,
Part Two"
(Pilot Episode)

# Appendix C
# Ratings Winners

Not all the Westerns were losers; a total of 24 different Westerns showed up in the final Nielsen ratings at the end of the season.

**1950–51**
7. "The Lone Ranger"
9. "Hopalong Cassidy"

**1956–57**
8. "Gunsmoke"

**1957–58**
1. "Gunsmoke"
3. "Tales of Wells Fargo"
4. "Have Gun, Will Travel"
6. "The Life and Legend of Wyatt Earp"
8. "The Restless Gun"
13. "Cheyenne"
21. "Dick Powell's Zane Grey Theatre"
23. "Wagon Train"
24. "Sugarfoot"

**1958–59**
1. "Gunsmoke"
2. "Wagon Train"
3. "Have Gun, Will Travel"
4. "The Rifleman"
6. "Maverick"

7. "Tales of Wells Fargo"
10. "The Life and Legend of Wyatt Earp"
13. "Dick Powell's Zane Grey Theatre"
15. "The Texan"
16. "Wanted: Dead or Alive"
18. "Cheyenne"
21. "Sugarfoot"

**1959–60**
1. "Gunsmoke"
2. "Wagon Train"
3. "Have Gun, Will Travel"
9. "Wanted: Dead or Alive"
14. "The Rifleman"
16. "The Lawman"
18. "Cheyenne"
19. "Rawhide"
20. "Maverick"
21. "The Life and Legend of Wyatt Earp"

**1960–61**
1. "Gunsmoke"
2. "Wagon Train"

3. "Have Gun, Will Travel"
6. "Rawhide"
17. "Bonanza"

**1961–62**
1. "Wagon Train"
2. "Bonanza"
3. "Gunsmoke"
13. "Rawhide"

**1962–63**
4. "Bonanza"
10. "Gunsmoke"
22. "Rawhide"
25. "Wagon Train"

**1963–64**
2. "Bonanza"
17. "The Virginian"
20. "Gunsmoke"

**1964–65**
1. "Bonanza"
14. "Branded"
22. "The Virginian"

**1965–66**
1. "Bonanza"
23. "The Wild, Wild West"
25. "The Virginian"

**1966–67**
1. "Bonanza"
11. "The Virginian"
25. "Daniel Boone"

**1967–68**
4. "Gunsmoke"
6. "Bonanza"
14. "The Virginian"

**1968–69**
3. "Bonanza"
6. "Gunsmoke"
17. "The Virginian"
21. "Daniel Boone"

**1969–70**
2. "Gunsmoke"
3. "Bonanza"

**1970–71**
5. "Gunsmoke"
9. "Bonanza"
18. "The Men from Shiloh"

**1971–72**
4. "Gunsmoke"
20. "Bonanza"

**1972–73**
8. "Gunsmoke"

**1973–74**
15. "Gunsmoke"

**1977–78**
11. "How the West Was Won"

# Comparative Ratings

Here's how the Westerns listed above stack up against each other in ratings:*

1. "Gunsmoke"**
2. "Bonanza"
3. "Wagon Train"
4. "Have Gun, Will Travel"

5. "The Virginian"†
6. "Rawhide"
7. "Tales of Wells Fargo"
8. "The Life and Legend of Wyatt Earp"
9. "The Rifleman"
10. "Cheyenne"
11. "Wanted: Dead or Alive"
12. "Maverick"
13. "The Lone Ranger"
14. "The Restless Gun"
15. "Dick Powell's Zane Grey Theatre"
16. "Hopalong Cassidy"
17. "How the West Was Won"
18. "Branded"
19. "The Texan"
20. "The Lawman"
21. "The Men from Shiloh"†
22. "Sugarfoot"
23. "Daniel Boone"
24. "The Wild, Wild West"

*Walt Disney series such as "Davy Crockett" and others were not considered since they did not constitute a regular series.

**"Gunsmoke" was television's all-time ratings leader.

†Although they were considered as two different series, "The Virginian" and "The Men from Shiloh" were essentially the same series with different titles.

# Appendix D
# Series by Other Names

If you've seen a show under a different title and haven't found it in this book, you may have seen it in syndication, where a title change was often made.

| Network | Syndication |
|---|---|
| "Black Saddle" | "The Westerners" |
| "Johnny Ringo" | "The Westerners" |
| "The Legend of Jesse James" | "Jesse James" |
| "Custer" | "Legend of Custer" |
| "Wagon Train" | "Major Adams, Trailmaster" |
| "The Westerner" | "The Westerners" |
| "Tales of Wells Fargo" | "Wells Fargo" |
| "Law of the Plainsman" | "The Westerners" |
| "The Rifleman" and | |
| "Dick Powell's Zane Grey Theatre" | "The Western Hour" |

# Appendix E
# Air Times

Dates shown are for the first and last network airing even if the series had ended its regular network run several years earlier. All times EST.

### The Adventures of Davy Crockett
| | | |
|---|---|---|
| 1954–55 | Wed. 7:30–8:30 | ABC |

### The Adventures of Jim Bowie
| | | |
|---|---|---|
| Sept. 7, 1956–Aug. 29, 1958 | Fri. 8:00–8:30 | ABC |

### The Adventures of Rin Tin Tin
| | | |
|---|---|---|
| Oct. 15, 1954–Aug. 28, 1959 | Fri. 7:30–8:00 | ABC |

### The Alaskans
| | | |
|---|---|---|
| Oct. 4, 1959–Sept. 25, 1960 | Sun. 9:30 –10:30 | ABC |

### Alias Smith and Jones
| | | |
|---|---|---|
| Jan. 21, 1971–Sept. 1971 | Thur. 7:30–8:30 | ABC |
| Sept. 1971–Aug. 1972 | Thur. 8:00–9:00 | |
| Sept. 1972–Jan. 13, 1973 | Sat. 8:00–9:00 | |

### The Americans
| | | |
|---|---|---|
| Jan. 23, 1961–Sept. 11, 1961 | Mon. 7:30–8:30 | NBC |

### The Barbary Coast
| | | |
|---|---|---|
| Sept. 8, 1975–Oct. 1975 | Mon. 8:00–9:00 | ABC |
| Oct. 1975–Jan. 9, 1976 | Fri. 8:00–9:00 | |

**Bat Masterson**

| | | |
|---|---|---|
| Oct. 8, 1958–Sept. 1959 | Wed. 9:30–10:00 | NBC |
| Oct. 1959–Sept. 1960 | Thur. 8:00–8:30 | |
| Sept. 1960–Sept. 21, 1961 | Thur. 8:30–9:00 | |

**The Big Valley**

| | | |
|---|---|---|
| Sept. 15, 1965–July 1966 | Wed. 9:00–10:00 | ABC |
| July 1966–May 19, 1969 | Mon. 10:00–11:00 | |

**Black Saddle**

| | | |
|---|---|---|
| Jan. 10, 1959–Sept. 1959 | Sat. 9:00–9:30 | NBC |
| Oct. 1959–Sept. 30, 1960 | Fri. 10:30–11:00 | ABC |

**Bonanza**

| | | |
|---|---|---|
| Sept. 12, 1959–Sept. 1961 | Sat. 7:30–8:30 | NBC |
| Sept. 1961–Sept. 1972 | Sun. 9:00–10:00 | |
| May 1972–Aug. 1972 | Tue. 7:30–8:30 | |
| Sept. 1972–Jan. 16, 1973 | Tue. 8:00–9:00 | |

**Branded**

| | | |
|---|---|---|
| Jan. 24, 1965–Sept. 4, 1966 | Sun. 8:30–9:00 | NBC |

**Brave Eagle**

| | | |
|---|---|---|
| Sept. 28, 1955–June 6, 1956 | Wed. 7:30–8:00 | CBS |

**Broken Arrow**

| | | |
|---|---|---|
| Sept. 25, 1956–Sept. 1958 | Tue. 9:00–9:30 | ABC |
| April 1960–Sept. 18, 1960 | Sun. 7:00–7:30 | |

**Bronco**

| | | |
|---|---|---|
| Sept. 23, 1958–Sept. 1960 | Tue. 7:30–8:30 | |
| Oct. 1960–Aug. 20, 1962 | Mon. 7:30–8:30 | |

**Buckskin**

| | | |
|---|---|---|
| July 3, 1958–Sept. 1958 | Thur. 9:30–10:00 | NBC |
| Oct. 1958–Jan. 1959 | Fri. 7:30–8:00 | |
| Jan. 1959 Sept. 1959 | Mon. 7:30–8:00 | |
| July 1965–Aug. 29, 1965 | Sun. 8:30–9:00 | |

**The Californians**

| | | |
|---|---|---|
| Sept. 24, 1957–March 1959 | Tue. 10:00–10:30 | NBC |
| April 1959–June 1959 | Tue. 9:00–9:30 | |
| July 1959–Aug. 27, 1959 | Thur. 7:30–8:00 | |

## Cheyenne

| Sept. 20, 1955–Sept. 1959 | Tue. 7:30–8:30 | ABC |
| Sept. 1959–Dec. 1962 | Mon. 7:30–8:30 | |
| April 1963–Sept. 13, 1963 | Fri. 7:30–8:30 | |

## Cimarron City

| Oct. 11, 1958–Sept. 1959 | Sat. 9:30–10:30 | NBC |
| June 1960–Sept. 16, 1960 | Fri. 7:30–8:30 | |

## Cimarron Strip

| Sept. 7, 1967–Sept. 1968 | Thur. 7:30–9:00 | CBS |
| July 1971–Sept. 7, 1971 | Tue. 8:30–10:00 | |

## Colt .45

| Oct. 18, 1957–Dec. 1957 | Fri. 10:00–10:30 | ABC |
| Jan. 1958–April 1958 | Fri. 8:30–9:00 | |
| Oct. 1958–Sept. 1959 | Sun. 9:00–9:30 | |
| Oct. 1959–March 1960 | Sun. 7:00–7:30 | |
| April 1960–Sept. 27, 1960 | Tue. 9:30–10:00 | |

## Cowboy in Africa

| Sept. 11, 1967–Sept. 16, 1968 | Mon. 7:30–8:30 | ABC |

## Cowboy Theatre

| June 9, 1957–Sept. 15, 1957 | Sun. 6:30–7:30 | NBC |

## The Cowboys

| Feb. 6, 1974–Aug. 14, 1974 | Wed. 8:00–8:30 | ABC |

## Custer

| Sept. 6, 1967–Dec. 27, 1967 | Wed. 7:30–8:30 | ABC |

## The Dakotas

| Jan. 7, 1963–Sept. 9, 1963 | Mon. 7:30–8:30 | ABC |

## Daniel Boone

| Sept. 24, 1964–Aug. 27, 1970 | Thur. 7:30–8:30 | NBC |

## The Deputy

| Sept. 12, 1959–Sept. 16, 1961 | Sat. 9:00–9:30 | NBC |

## Destry

| Feb. 14, 1964–Sept. 11, 1964 | Fri. 7:30–8:30 | ABC |

### Dick Powell's Zane Grey Theatre
| | | |
|---|---|---|
| Oct. 5, 1956–July 1958 | Fri. 8:30–9:00 | CBS |
| Oct. 1958–Sept. 1960 | Thur. 9:00–9:30 | |
| Oct. 1960–July 1961 | Thur. 8:30–9:00 | |
| April 1962–Sept. 20, 1962 | Thur. 9:30–10:00 | |

### Dirty Sally
| | | |
|---|---|---|
| Jan. 11, 1974–July 19, 1974 | Fri. 8:00–8:30 | CBS |

### Dundee and the Culhane
| | | |
|---|---|---|
| Sept. 6, 1967–Dec. 13, 1967 | Wed. 10:00–11:00 | CBS |

### Empire
| | | |
|---|---|---|
| Sept. 25, 1962–Sept. 1963 | Tue. 8:30–9:30 | NBC |
| March 1964–Sept. 6, 1964 | Sun. 7:30–8:30 | ABC |

### Frontier
| | | |
|---|---|---|
| Sept. 25, 1955–Sept. 9, 1956 | Sun. 7:30–8:00 | NBC |

### Frontier Circus
| | | |
|---|---|---|
| Oct. 5, 1961–Jan. 1962 | Thur. 7:30–8:30 | CBS |
| Feb. 1962–Sept. 1962 | Thur. 8:00–9:00 | |
| Sept. 20, 1962 | Thur. 7:30–8:30 | |

### Frontier Justice
| | | |
|---|---|---|
| July 7, 1958–Sept. 1958 | Mon. 9:30–10:00 | CBS |
| July 1959–Sept. 1959 | Mon. 9:00–9:30 | |
| Aug. 1961–Sept. 28, 1961 | Thur. 8:30–9:00 | |

### The Gene Autry Show
| | | |
|---|---|---|
| July 23, 1950–July 1953 | Mon. 9:30–10:00 | CBS |
| July 1953–Sept. 1954 | Tue. 8:00–8:30 | |
| Sept. 1954–Aug. 7, 1956 | Sat. 7:00–7:30 | |

### The Guns of Will Sonnett
| | | |
|---|---|---|
| Sept. 8, 1967–May 1969 | Fri. 9:30–10:00 | ABC |
| June 1969–Sept. 15, 1969 | Mon. 8:30–9:00 | |

### Gunslinger
| | | |
|---|---|---|
| Feb. 9, 1961–Sept. 14, 1961 | Thur. 9:00–10:00 | CBS |

### Gunsmoke
| | | |
|---|---|---|
| Sept. 10, 1955–Sept. 1961 | Sat. 10:00–10:30 | CBS |

| Sept. 1961–Sept. 1967 | Sat. 10:00–11:00 | |
| Oct. 1961–June 1964 | Tue. 7:30–8:00 | |
| Sept. 1967–Sept. 1971 | Mon. 7:30–8:30 | |
| Sept. 1971–Sept. 1, 1975 | Mon. 8:00–9:00 | |

## Have Gun, Will Travel

| Sept. 14, 1957–Sept. 21, 1963 | Sat. 9:30–10:00 | CBS |

## Hec Ramsey

| Oct. 8, 1972–Aug. 25, 1974 | Sun. 8:30–10:00 | NBC |

## The High Chaparral

| Sept. 10, 1967–Sept. 1968 | Sun. 10:00–11:00 | |
| Sept. 1968–Dec. 1970 | Fri. 7:30–8:30 | |
| Feb. 1971–Sept. 10, 1971 | Fri. 7:30–8:30 | |

## Hondo

| Sept. 8, 1967–Dec. 29, 1967 | Fri. 8:30–9:30 | ABC |

## Hopalong Cassidy

| June 24, 1949–Oct. 1949 | Fri. 8:00–9:00 | NBC |
| April 1950–Dec. 23, 1951 | Sun. 6:00–7:00 | |

## Hotel de Paree

| Oct. 2, 1959–Sept. 23, 1960 | Fri. 8:30–9:00 | CBS |

## How the West Was Won

| Feb. 12, 1978–May 1978 | Sun. 8:00–9:00 | ABC |
| July 1978–Aug. 28, 1978 | Sun. 8:00–9:00 | |

## The Iron Horse

| Sept. 12, 1966–Sept. 1967 | Mon. 7:30–8:30 | ABC |
| Sept. 1967–Jan. 6, 1968 | Sat. 9:30–10:30 | |

## Jefferson Drum

| April 25, 1958–Sept. 1958 | Fri. 8:00–8:30 | NBC |
| Sept. 1958–Oct. 1958 | Fri. 7:30–8:00 | |
| Oct. 1958–April 23, 1959 | Thur. 7:30–8:00 | |

## Johnny Ringo

| Oct. 1, 1959–Sept. 29, 1960 | Thur. 8:30–9:00 | CBS |

**Klondike**

Oct. 10, 1960–Feb. 6, 1961              Mon. 9:00–9:30              NBC

**Kung Fu**

Oct. 14, 1972–Nov. 1972               Sat. 8:00–9:00              ABC
Jan. 1973–Aug. 1974                   Thur. 9:00–10:00
Sept. 1974–Oct. 1974                  Sat. 9:00–10:00
Nov. 1974–Jan. 1975                   Fri. 8:00–9:00
Jan. 1975–June 28, 1975               Sat. 8:00–9:00

**Lancer**

Sept. 24, 1968–June 1970              Tue. 7:30–8:30              CBS
May 1971–Sept. 9, 1971                Thur. 8:00–9:00

**Laramie**

Sept. 15, 1959–Sept. 17, 1963         Tue. 7:30–8:30              NBC

**Laredo**

Sept. 16, 1965–Sept. 1966             Thur. 8:30–9:30             NBC
Sept. 1966–Sept. 1, 1967              Fri. 10:00–11:00

**Law of the Plainsman**

Oct. 1, 1959–Sept. 1960               Thur. 7:30–8:00             NBC
July 1962–Sept. 24, 1962              Mon. 8:30–9:00              ABC

**The Lawman**

Oct. 5, 1958–April 1962               Sun. 8:30–9:00              ABC
April 1962–Oct. 2, 1962               Sun. 10:30–11:00

**The Legend of Jesse James**

Sept. 13, 1965–Sept. 5, 1966          Mon. 8:30–9:00              ABC

**The Life and Legend of Wyatt Earp**

Sept. 6, 1955–Sept. 26, 1961          Tue. 8:30–9:00              ABC

**The Life and Times of Grizzly Adams**

Feb 9, 1977–July 26, 1978             Wed. 8:00–9:00              NBC

**The Lone Ranger**

Sept. 15, 1949–Sept. 1957             Thur. 7:30–8:00             ABC
June 1950–Sept. 12, 1950              Fri. 10:00–10:30

**The Loner**

Sept. 18, 1965–April 30, 1966         Sat. 9:30–10:00             CBS

## A Man Called Shenandoah
Sept. 13, 1965–Sept. 5, 1966          Mon. 9:00–9:30              ABC

## The Man from Blackhawk
Oct. 9, 1959–Sept. 23, 1960          Fri. 8:30–9:00              ABC

## The Marshal of Gunsight Pass
March 12, 1950–Sept. 30, 1950          Sat. 6:30–7:00              ABC

## Maverick
Sept. 22, 1957–Sept. 1961          Sun. 7:30–8:30              ABC
Sept. 1961–July 8, 1962          Sun. 6:30–7:30

## The Men from Shiloh
See The Virginian

## The Monroes
Sept. 7, 1966–Aug. 30, 1967          Wed. 8:00–8:30              ABC

## The New Land
Sept. 14, 1974–Oct. 19, 1974          Sat. 8:00–9:00              ABC

## Nichols
Sept. 16, 1971–Nov. 1971          Thur. 9:00–10:00              NBC
Nov. 1971–Aug. 1, 1972          Tue. 9:30–10:30

## The Nine Lives of Elfego Baca
1958          Fri. 8:00–9:00              ABC

## Northwest Passage
Sept. 14, 1958–Jan. 1959          Sun. 7:30–8:00              NBC
Jan. 1959–Sept. 8, 1959          Fri. 7:30–8:00

## The Oregon Trail
Sept. 21, 1977–Oct. 26, 1977          Wed. 9:00–10:00              NBC

## The Outcasts
Sept. 23, 1968–Sept. 15, 1969          Mon. 9:00–10:00              ABC

## The Outlaws
Sept. 29, 1960–Sept. 13, 1962          Thur. 7:30–8:30              NBC

## The Overland Trail
Feb. 7, 1960–Sept. 11, 1960          Sun. 7:00–8:00              NBC

## Pall Mall Playhouse

July 20, 1955–Sept. 7, 1955          Wed. 8:30–9:00          ABC

## The Quest

Sept. 22, 1976–Dec. 29, 1976          Wed. 10:00–11:00          NBC

## Rawhide

| | | |
|---|---|---|
| Jan. 9, 1959–April 1959 | Fri. 8:00–9:00 | CBS |
| May 1959–Sept. 1963 | Fri. 7:30–8:30 | |
| Sept. 1963–Sept. 1964 | Thur. 8:00–9:00 | |
| Sept. 1964–Sept. 1965 | Fri. 7:30–8:30 | |
| Sept. 1965–Jan. 4, 1966 | Tue. 7:30–8:30 | |

## The Rebel

| | | |
|---|---|---|
| Oct. 4, 1959–Sept. 1961 | Sun. 9:00–9:30 | ABC |
| June 1962–Sept. 12, 1962 | Wed. 8:30–9:00 | NBC |

## Redigo

Sept. 24, 1963–Dec. 31, 1963          Tue. 8:30–9:00          NBC

## The Restless Gun

Sept. 23, 1957–Sept. 14, 1959          Mon. 8:00–8:30          NBC

## The Rifleman

| | | |
|---|---|---|
| Sept. 30, 1958–Sept. 1960 | Tue. 9:00–9:30 | ABC |
| Sept. 1960–Sept. 1961 | Tue. 8:00–8:30 | |
| Oct. 1961–July 1, 1963 | Mon. 8:30–9:00 | |

## Riverboat

| | | |
|---|---|---|
| Sept. 13, 1959–Jan. 1960 | Sun. 7:00–8:00 | NBC |
| Feb. 1960–Jan. 16, 1961 | Mon. 7:30–8:30 | |

## The Road West

Sept. 12, 1966–Aug. 28, 1967          Mon. 9:00–10:00          NBC

## The Rough Riders

Oct. 2, 1958–Sept. 24, 1959          Thur. 9:30–10:00          ABC

## The Roy Rogers Show

| | | |
|---|---|---|
| Dec. 30, 1951–June 1952 | Sun. 6:30–7:00 | NBC |
| Aug. 1952–June 23, 1957 | Sun. 6:30–7:00 | |

## The Saga of Andy Burnette

1958          Fri. 8:00–9:00          CBS

## Sara
Feb. 13, 1976–July 30, 1976              Fri. 8:00–9:00              CBS

## Saturday Roundup
June 10, 1951–Sept. 1, 1951             Sat. 8:00–9:00              NBC

## Sergeant Preston of the Yukon
Sept. 29, 1955–Sept. 25, 1958           Thur. 7:30–8:00            CBS

## Shane
Sept. 10, 1966–Dec. 31, 1966            Sat. 7:30–8:30             ABC

## Sky King
Sept. 21, 1953–Sept. 1954               Mon. 8:00–8:30             ABC
Aug. 1954–Sept. 12, 1954                Sun. 6:00–6:30

## Stagecoach West
Oct. 4, 1960–Sept. 26, 1961             Tue. 9:00–10:00            ABC

## The Swamp Fox
1958                                    Sun. 6:30–7:30             ABC

## Sugarfoot
Sept. 17, 1957–Sept. 1960               Tue. 7:30–8:30             ABC
Oct. 1960–July 3, 1961                  Mon. 7:30–8:30

## Tales of the Texas Rangers
1955–1958                               Afternoons                CBS
Oct. 1958–Dec. 1958                     Thur. 5:00–5:30            ABC
Dec. 22, 1958–May 25, 1959             Mon. 7:30–8:00             ABC

## Tales of Wells Fargo
March 18, 1957–Sept. 1961              Mon. 8:30–9:00             NBC
Sept. 1961–Sept. 8, 1962               Sat. 7:30–8:30

## The Tall Man
Sept. 10, 1960–Sept. 1, 1962           Sat. 8:30–9:00             NBC

## Tate
June 8, 1960–Sept. 28, 1960            Wed. 9:30–10:00            NBC

## Temple Houston
Sept. 19, 1963–Sept. 10, 1964          Thur. 7:30–8:30     8:30   NBC

### The Texan
Sept. 29, 1958–Sept. 12, 1960          Mon. 8:00–8:30                    CBS

### Tombstone Territory
Oct. 16, 1957–Sept. 1958             Fri. 8:00–8:30                    ABC
March 1959–Oct. 9, 1959              Fri. 9:00–9:30

### Trackdown
Oct. 4, 1957–Jan. 1959               Fri. 8:00–8:30                    CBS
Feb. 1959–Sept. 23, 1959             Wed. 8:30–9:00

### The Travels of Jamie McPheeters
Sept. 15, 1963–March 15, 1964        Sun. 7:30–8:30                    ABC

### The Virginian
Sept. 19, 1962–Sept. 8, 1971         Wed. 7:30–9:00                    NBC
Series aired as *The Men from Shiloh* in its final season.

### Wagon Train
Sept. 18, 1957–Sept. 1962            Wed. 7:30–8:30                    NBC
Sept. 1962–Sept. 1963                Wed. 7:30–8:30                    ABC
Sept. 1963–Sept. 1964                Mon. 8:30–10:00
Sept. 1964–Sept. 5, 1965             Sun. 7:30–8:30

### Westward Ho! The Wagons
1959

### Wanted: Dead or Alive
Sept. 6, 1958–Sept. 1960             Sat. 8:30–9:00                    CBS
Sept. 1960–March 29, 1961            Wed. 8:30–9:00

### The Westerner
Sept. 30, 1960–Dec. 30, 1960         Fri. 8:30–9:00                    NBC

### Whispering Smith
May 15, 1961–Sept. 18, 1961          Mon. 9:00–9:30                    NBC

### Wichita Town
Sept. 30, 1959–April 1960            Wed. 10:30–11:00                  NBC
June 1960–Sept. 23, 1960             Fri. 8:30–9:00

### The Wide Country
Sept. 20, 1962–Sept. 12, 1963        Thur. 7:30–8:30                   NBC

## The Wild Wild West

Sept. 17, 1965–Sept. 1969          Fri. 7:30–8:30          CBS
July 1970–Sept. 7, 1970           Mon. 10:00–11:00

## Wrangler

Aug. 4, 1960–Sept. 15, 1960        Thur. 9:30–10:00        NBC

## Yancy Derringer

Oct. 2, 1958–Sept. 24, 1959        Thur. 8:30–9:00         CBS

## Young Dan'l Boone

Sept. 12, 1977                     Mon. 8:00–9:00          CBS
Oct. 4, 1977                       Tue. 8:00–9:00

## Zorro

Oct. 10, 1957–Sept. 24, 1959       Thur. 8:00–8:30         ABC

# Index

## A

Aaker, Lee 14
"ABC Movie of the Week" 15, 58
"Acapulco" 51, 58
Adams, Doc 45
Adams, Grizzly 66
Adams, Nick 79
Adams, Major Seth 103
Adams, Shank 23
Adams, Stanley 37, 38
"The Adventures of Davy Crockett"
    9–12, 75
"The Adventures of Frontier Fremont,"
    66
"The Adventures of Jim Bowie" 12, 13,
    22
"The Adventures of Kit Carson" 13, 14
"The Adventures of Rin Tin Tin," 14
Ahn, Philip 59
"The Alaskans" 14, 15
"Alias Smith and Jones" 15, 16, 80
Allen, Vernett, III 101
"America After Dark" 5
"The Americans" 16
Ames, Ed 36, 37
Anderson, Annie 35
Anderson, Donna 101
Anderson, John 64
Anderson, Michael, Jr. 73
Andrews, Tod 44
"Annie Oakley" 16, 17
Ansara, Michael 24, 25, 61
Appleseed, Johnny 12
Arden, Eve 18, 70
"Armstrong Circle Theatre" 6
Arness, James 2, 5, 45, 46, 54
Arnold, Elliott 24

"Arrest and Trial" 23, 82
Arvan, Jan 113
Asper, Quint 46
"Assignment Vienna" 110
Ates, Roscoe 71
Audubon, John James 12
Autry, Gene 17, 42, 43, 44, 85
Ayres, Lew 42

## B

"Baa Baa Black Sheep" 110
Baca, Elfego 10
Baggott, Shep 101
Bailey, George 87
Bailey, Julia 88
"The Ballad of Davy Crockett" 11, 12
"The Ballad of Paladin" 49
Bannon, Race 27
"The Barbary Coast" 5, 18
Bardette, Trevor 64
Barkley, Audra 19
Barkley, Heath 19
Barkley, Jarrod 19
Barkley, Nick 19, 21
Barkley, Victoria 19
"Barnaby Jones" 75
Barry, Gene 18
Barstow, Claude 87
"Bat Masterson" 18, 19
"Battlestar Galactica" 22
Baur, Elizabeth 59
Baylor, Hal 64
Bean, Judge Roy 57
The Beatles 2

## C

Purcell, Beth 30
Purdy, Alice 30
Purdy, Burt 30
Pyle, Denver 64, 66

## Q

"The Quest" 78
Quince, Jim 79
Quine, Don 102

## R

Ragan, Frank 36
Raines, Steve 79
Rambo, Dack 40, 44
Ramos, Rudy 50
Ramsey, Hec 49
Randall, Josh 105
Randall, Stuart 30, 60
Random, Bob 55
"The Range Rider" 78, 111
"The Rat Patrol" 2
"Rawhide" 78, 79, 83
Reagan, Ronald 37, 38, 104
"The Real McCoys" 44
"The Rebel" 79, 80
Redford, Robert 15
Redigo, Jim 41, 80
"Redigo" 80
Reid, John 67
Renaldo, Duncan 31
"The Restless Gun" 80, 81, 82, 96
Reynolds, Bob 43
Reynolds, Burt 46, 83
Reynolds, Elizabeth 84
Rhoades, Dusty 22
"Rich Man, Poor Man" 63
Richards, Addison 30
Richards, Jeff 55, 56
"The Rifleman" 23, 81, 83
Riley, Chester A. 2, 77, 91
Riley, Joe 61
Rin Tin Tin 14
Ringo, Johnny 56, 57, 64
"Riverboat" 83
Road, Michael 27
"The Road West" 84, 85
"The Roaring Twenties" 15, 27
"The Robe" 101

Roberts, Pernell 20
Robertson, Dale 55, 96
Rockford, James 73
Rockford, Matthew 30
"The Rockford Files" 72, 73, 75
Rockwell, Robert 69, 70
Rodriguez, Rico 107
Rogers, Barnabas 55
Rogers, Robert 75
Rogers, Roy 42, 85, 86, 87 see also
   Evans, Dale
Rogers, Wayne 91
Rogers, Will, Jr. 77
Romack, George 107
Romero, Carlos 107
"Room for One More" 60
"Roots" 69
Roter, Diane 102
"The Rough Riders" 84
"The Rounders" 41
"Roy Rogers and Dale Evans" 84
"The Roy Rogers Show" 84, 85, 86, 87
Rucker, Dennis 49
Rudley, Herbert 28
Russell, Georgie 10, 11
Russell, John 62
Russell, Kitty 4, 45, 46, 47
Russell, Kurt 74, 78, 100
Ryan, Rebecca 111
Ryker, Emmett 102
Ryker, Rufe 90
Rynning, Tom 101

## S

"The Saga of Andy Burnette" 7, 10, 87,
   88
"The Saint" 73
St. Jacques, Raymond 79
St. James, Susan 49
Salmi, Albert 36
Sampson, Art 30
Sanford, Ralph 64
"San Francisco International Airport" 69
Santa Ana 10
"Sara" 87, 88
"Saturday Roundup" 88, 89
Sawyer, Joe 14
Scarlett, Joe 79
"Schlitz Playhouse of Stars" 32, 81, 96
Schreck, Vicki 54
Schultz, Keith 73
Schultz, Kevin 73